MY FIRST BOOK OF
ANIMALS

Monica Harris
Mark Rosenthal, Consultant

pil

Publications International, Ltd.

Writer: Monica Harris is a freelance writer who has written several educational books including *Tarantulas, Walking Sticks,* and *Black Widow Spiders.* In addition, she has written articles for magazines such as *Good Apple Newspaper* and *Highlights* magazine.

Consultant: Mark Rosenthal has contributed to many zoological publications as both a writer and a consultant. He is a curator at the Lincoln Park Zoo in Chicago, IL, and holds a Master of Arts in Zoology.

Illustrator: James Mravec

CONTENTS

CURIOUS ABOUT ANIMALS

Are you curious about the animals around you? Do you look for bugs under logs or peek inside holes to see if an animal lives there? Are you intrigued with the way animals eat and mesmerized with how mother animals care for their young? Do you ask yourself: *How does a snake swallow its food whole? How far can a flea jump?*

Boa Constrictor

What's the difference between an alligator and a crocodile? An excellent source for answering some of your questions is *My First Book of Animals.*

From the tiniest flea to the largest whale, animals have adapted for survival in their habitats. Some are covered by fur or feathers; others have thick shells or scales; and still others have body parts that are hardly recognizable! Even within an animal group, there can be differences. Birds, for example, have different

Zebras

Whale

shaped feet depending on where and how they live.

Adaptation has brought diversity and efficiency to the animal kingdom. Zebras survive in the heat of Africa's savannas, macaws fly gracefully through the thick rainforest jungles, and eerie viperfish endure in the cold, dark depths of the ocean.

You will be amazed at how animals protect themselves. Through beautiful illustrations you will see how some animals, like the elephant, use size to ward off danger. Smaller animals, like the fire ant, have developed other methods, such as painful stings, that keep predators at bay. There are even animals that mimic more dangerous species in coloration or behavior. They fool their enemies in the hope that they won't be the next meal.

Elephant

The feeding behavior of animals is crucial to the balance of nature. You will discover what animals eat and how they get their food. Owls, eels, chameleons, and tarantulas are all hunters, but they use different techniques. Insects have specially shaped mouth parts depending on what they feed on. There are even species of ants that cultivate their own food.

In easy-to-understand diagrams, you will see the reproductive cycles of several animals. Many, like dolphins and wolves, give birth to live young. Birds, fish, frogs, and turtles lay eggs from which their babies are hatched. Some lay hard-shell eggs while others' eggs are just jellylike sacs.

Each chapter begins with the major physical and behavioral characteristics of a specific animal group. From there, the animals are broken down into more precise subgroups. Here, you have an opportunity to

Butterfly

Wolf

Frog

Chameleon

Cat

learn about individual species and some of the things that make them special. Subjects that require a more thorough description are found in sidebars. They focus on such areas as the metamorphosis of a butterfly, the patterns of cat fur, or the differences between horns and antlers.

Tarantula

My First Book of Animals provides a great opportunity to learn about the diversity of life while satisfying your curiosity. In doing so, you get a better appreciation of your world and a greater understanding of the animals that live in it.

MARVELOUS MAMMALS

About 4,000 different types of mammals live throughout the world. We humans belong to this group. In fact, mammals dwell on land, in the water, and even in the air. They can be as small as a mouse or as large as a whale.

Mammals share certain features. They all have hair or fur on their bodies. They all have a backbone. And they all are warm-blooded. That means they keep their body temperature the same no matter how cold or how hot it is outside their bodies.

Most mammals give birth to babies, but a few mammals lay eggs. All female mammals feed milk to their young. They make milk in special body parts called "mammary glands."

Mammals can be carnivores (meateaters), herbivores (planteaters), or omnivores (meat- and planteaters). For example, lions are carnivores, rabbits are herbivores, and humans are omnivores.

Domestic Dogs

Dogs were domesticated, or tamed, about 12,000 years ago. Ever since then, dogs have lived with people. Dogs have been companions with humans longer than any other animal in the world. Today, there are 400 different dog breeds, and they are relatives of the wolf. Dogs keep us company as pets. They help protect our homes and farms. They help people in trouble. For example, Bernese Mountain Dogs rescue people trapped in the snow. Dogs even help humans with disabilities. Labrador retrievers are excellent guide dogs for the blind.

Standard Poodle Poodles, which vary in size from standard to miniature, were first used as hunting dogs because of their high intelligence. When hunters killed birds and the birds fell into a lake, poodles would swim out to fetch them.

German Shepherd The German shepherd is one of the most recognized breeds in the world. They are easy to train and can be used as herding dogs, guard dogs, and guide dogs.

Greyhound The greyhound is one of the fastest dogs. They love to chase things like rabbits. Their long legs and thin bodies make them great runners.

Dachshund Dachshunds are often called wiener dogs because they look like hot dogs with legs! Dachshunds were once used to hunt animals in burrows and tunnels.

Cocker Spaniel Cocker spaniels have large, droopy ears and lots of hair. Their fur needs to be brushed often, or it will get badly knotted.

Golden Retriever Golden retrievers have beautiful gold-colored fur. They are currently one of the most popular dogs because they are gentle and easy to train.

Wild Canines

Since domestic dogs came from wild dogs, they both look alike. Wild dogs, however, are just that—wild! They are usually afraid of humans and stay away from them whenever possible. Wild dogs cannot be trained. Many wild dogs live in groups called "packs," which are made of many family groups and usually have one leader. Wild dogs use their sense of smell and sharp hearing to find their prey. Packs that hunt together have an easier time killing larger animals, such as antelope or zebras. Wild dogs are carnivores, which means they eat meat. They have long front teeth for tearing meat. Wider, sharp teeth in the back are used for slicing meat into smaller pieces.

Timber Wolf The timber wolf, or gray wolf, is the largest member of the wild dog family. Wolves are known for their howling, which is their way of talking to each other.

Dingo Dingoes are wild dogs found in Australia. They look like domestic dogs, but your pet dog can do one thing the dingo can't do—bark!

Red Fox The red fox usually hunts alone. It is nocturnal, which means it hunts at night. It has red-dish colored fur, and its tail has a white tip.

Coyote Coyotes eat all kinds of food, including snakes, insects, fruits, and dead animals. For many years, farmers have hunted coyotes because they killed their cattle.

Arctic Fox

Domestic Cats

Just as domestic dogs came from wild dogs, domestic cats came from wildcats. Scientists believe the African wildcat was tamed about 4,000 years ago in ancient Egypt. Today, there are more than 40 different breeds of cats. Cats make good pets because they are quiet and friendly. They usually like to be touched and stroked. Cats are also clean pets. They groom themselves by licking their fur with a rough tongue. It's like using a hairbrush to get rid of tangles! Cats can also be trained to use a litter box. Even though humans feed their cats, they are still hunters. They use their keen eyesight and hearing to find birds and mice. Pads on the bottom of their feet allow them to sneak up on their prey. Using quick muscles and sharp claws, they pounce on their unsuspecting victim.

Sphinx To most people, the sphinx cat looks rather strange. It is called "a hairless cat." It really does have hair, but it's fine and soft. A sphinx feels like a peach when you touch it.

Birman

Siamese Siamese cats have short, tan fur on their bodies and dark fur around their faces. Siamese cats have almond-shaped blue eyes.

Russian Blue The Russian blue has thick, short, silver-tipped gray fur.

Domestic cat fur patterns

Domestic cats come in a variety of sizes, colors, fur types, and patterns. Cats can have short hair or long hair. Persians are good examples of long-haired cats. Cats can come in solid colors or with a pattern in their fur. A cat that has striped fur is called a "tabby." A calico pattern has three separate colors of fur. The colors are usually black, red, and white.

long hair   *short hair*

tabby   *calico*

Persian Persian cats have a long, flowing coat and an expressive, flat face. They have soft voices and love to sit in the sun.

Wild Felines

When you think of wildcats, you probably think of lions and tigers. It's true that these are wildcats, but most wildcats are small. The rusty-spotted cat of India, for example, is only 14–18 inches long! Wildcats have thick fur coats that come in a variety of colors and patterns. The European wildcat lives in the forests of Asia, Europe, and Scotland. It is a tan color with dark stripes. This camouflages, or hides, it from its enemies and prey. Wildcats are well suited for living in their surroundings. Snow leopards have thick tails that keep them warm when they lie down. The fishing cat of India has partially webbed paws. This helps them to catch frogs and fish. All cats have great eyesight and keen hearing.

Siberian Tiger Tigers are the largest of the wildcats. Their dark stripes help them hide in the tall grasses of Asia.

Lion The lion is often called the "King of the Jungle," but it doesn't live there! Lions live in the plains and woodlands. Male lions have furry, dark manes around their faces. Females don't have manes.

Jaguar Jaguars are different from other cats because they like to go into the water. They are excellent swimmers and sometimes hunt river animals, such as turtles and otters.

Cheetah The cheetah is the fastest animal on land. It can run at a speed of about 60 mph! That's faster than many cars on the road.

Cougar

Leopard Leopards are strong and can easily climb trees. They carry their food into a tree so other animals can't steal it.

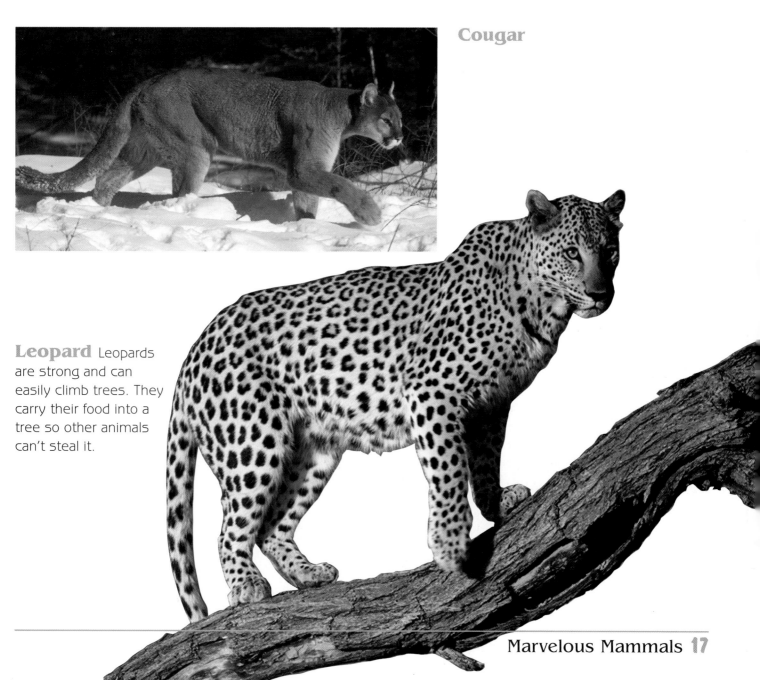

Riding Mammals and Bison

Many mammals are helpful to people. One working mammal is the horse. Horses are strong and fast. People have used domestic horses for more than 5,000 years. Humans ride on their backs or have them pull such things as coaches and carts. Camels are helpful in the world's driest places. They are often called "ships of the desert." This is because they can carry people or large amounts of cargo. Camels have wide feet that stop them from sinking into the sand. They can also close their nostrils to keep sand from getting into their noses. Camels can drink 15 gallons of water at one time and can go without water for up to 15 days. Donkeys can also carry people and cargo. They look similar to horses but have smaller hooves and thicker coats. This makes them perfect for working in dry, rocky areas.

Donkey Just like horses, donkeys walk on hooves. A donkey's hoof is a single toe. It is made of a thick material called keratin. Your fingernails are also made of keratin.

Camels A one-humped camel is called a "dromedary." A two-humped camel is a "bactrian." Humps are filled with fat, which helps camels live without food or water for days.

Horse There are more than 150 different types of horses in the world. Horses come in many colors. Each color has a special name. This horse is a chestnut.

The American bison

The American bison is North America's largest animal. It is also called the plains buffalo. Until the mid-1800s, the bison was the world's most plentiful grazing mammal. Close to 50 million grazed across the plains of the West. Unfortunately, in less than 50 years, the bison came close to extinction. Early settlers shot and killed all but about 1,000 of these animals. Luckily, bison are now protected and have increased in numbers. Most bison live in protected areas.

Other Hoofed Mammals

A hoof is a specially shaped toe. It can hold all of an animal's weight without breaking. The end of the hoof has a thick layer of keratin. Hooves may seem small, but they're strong. Hoofed mammals get a good grip on the ground, which allows them to run quickly. Scientists divide hoofed mammals into two groups. The largest group includes pigs, camels, deer, and giraffes. They are known as cloven-hoofed animals. This is because their hoof is split into two parts. The other group includes horses and rhinos. They have an uneven number of toes. It may be as few as one toe or as many as five.

Cattle The most common example of cattle is the cow. Cows are grazers, which means they feed on grass. Cows have four pockets in their stomachs for breaking down grass so they can digest it. They are also fed grains by farmers.

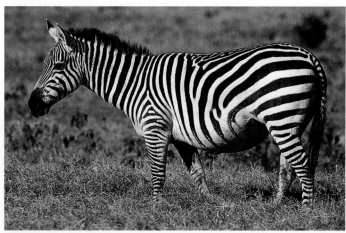

Zebra Zebras are wild horses found in Africa. Their black and white stripes protect them from predators. Each zebra has a different stripe pattern—just like a human fingerprint!

Bighorn Sheep Male bighorn sheep have large curved horns. Males run at each other and ram their horns together. The winner gets to be the leader of the herd.

Giraffe The giraffe is the world's tallest animal. Its long neck and legs help it reach leaves high in the trees. Giraffes can also see danger coming from far away.

Horns versus antlers

Many hoofed mammals have sharp things growing from the tops of their heads. Some are called "horns," and others are called "antlers." What's the difference? Horns are hard permanent structures that never fall off. They keep growing as long as the animal is alive. Animals like cows, sheep, goats, and antelopes have horns. Antlers are also hard growths, but they are not permanent. They fall off about once a year and grow back. Antlers can be branched. This means that they can have many spikes, or points, coming out of one main antler. Elk, deer, and moose are examples of animals with antlers.

White-tailed Deer White-tailed deer (above and right) run away and lift their tails up when they're scared. Their tail is brown on the top but white underneath. This warns other deer of danger.

Pachyderms

Pachyderms are mammals with thick skin and hoofed feet. They include the elephant, hippopotamus, and rhinoceros. Elephants are the heaviest land animals. An adult elephant can weigh more than six cars! Elephants are intelligent and can be trained to do heavy work, such as lifting logs or pulling out tree stumps. Elephants have long noses called "trunks." They use their trunks to put food and water into their mouths. You'll see some elephants with tusks. Tusks are teeth that grow outside of an animal's mouth.

Hippopotamuses, or hippos, spend most of the day in the water eating plants. Hippos have four webbed toes. They can close their nostrils so water doesn't get into their noses. Rhinoceroses, or rhinos, live on the open grasslands of Africa and in the forests of Asia. They have one or two sharp horns on their heads. The horns are actually made of the same material as your hair!

Hippopotamus When you search for a hippo, you may see only its eyes, nose, and ears sticking out of the water. Hippos stay in the water to keep cool and to protect their skin from sunburn.

Black Rhinoceros Black rhinoceroses live in Africa. They use a flexible, pointed upper lip to eat plants. Rhinos have poor eyesight and will charge at predators (other animals that try to kill them).

African Elephant The African elephant is the biggest species of elephant. It has large, round ears. Its trunk has two tips that are used like fingers to pick things up.

Asian Elephant Asian elephants are smaller than African elephants. Their ears are smaller, and their trunks have only one tip. They live mostly in the forest where they eat grass and leaves.

Two sizes of hippos

Two species of hippopotamus are the common hippo and the pygmy hippo. The common hippo lives around the waters in east and south Africa. They have large bodies with wide heads. They can be found living in herds. The pygmy hippo is much smaller. Found in West African tropical forests, its body and mouth are narrower. Pygmy hippos spend most of their time on land eating leaves. When threatened, they will run into the water.

pygmy hippo

common hippo

Marsupials

Marsupials are mammals that raise their babies inside a pouch. This includes kangaroos, wallabies, koalas, and opossum. When female marsupials give birth, the babies are tiny and hairless. They must crawl through their mother's fur to a pouch. When they get there, they hook their mouths onto a teat. Teats produce milk from special body parts called "mammary glands." The pouch is a safe place for babies to eat and grow. When the baby has grown large enough, it can go outside of the pouch. Kangaroo pouches have special muscles that tighten when the kangaroo hops. They squeeze the baby so it does not fall out! Koala and opossum babies ride on their mothers' backs when they can't fit in the pouch anymore.

Red Kangaroo The red kangaroo is the largest marsupial. It has huge feet for hopping and a thick tail for balancing. Red kangaroos cannot walk—only hop!

North American Opossum The opossum is the only marsupial that lives in America. It has a pointed snout and a long, bare tail. A young opossum can hang upside down by its tail.

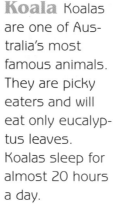

Koala Koalas are one of Australia's most famous animals. They are picky eaters and will eat only eucalyptus leaves. Koalas sleep for almost 20 hours a day.

Bats and Rodents

Almost 1,000 species of bats are found in the world. Bats are the only mammals that can fly. They have furry bodies, big ears, and wings that look like leather. If you look closely, you can see that their wings are made of skin stretched between long fingers. Many bats are nocturnal, which means they are active at night. Most bats feed on fruit, flowers, or insects.

Rodents are the largest group of mammals, with more than 1,600 species. This group includes squirrels, rats, and beavers. Rodents have sharp front teeth called incisors. These teeth never stop growing and are always sharp. Rodents use them to chew through roots, to dig underground, to open hard seeds, and even to cut down trees. Rodents do not have long lives. Rodents reproduce very quickly, sometimes giving birth to as many as one hundred babies a year!

Little Brown Bat Little brown bats are found all over the continental United States (not in Hawaii). They're about the size of your fist. Little brown bats eat insects that they catch in the air.

Vampire Bat Vampire bats make small cuts in the skin of animals. They drink the blood that comes out. Adult vampire bats drink about five teaspoons of blood a day.

Bats and Rodents

Eastern Chipmunk Eastern chipmunks are found in North America. They have dark stripes on their body and a small tail that flicks very quickly. Chipmunks store extra food in underground burrows.

Black-tailed Prairie Dog The black-tailed prairie dog is not really a dog! It's a large squirrel that lives underground. To warn each other of danger, prairie dogs make a loud barking noise.

Harvest Mouse The harvest mouse, or field mouse, spends its life in open fields eating seeds and small insects. Harvest mice have long tails covered with really fine hair.

Eastern Gray Squirrel

Porcupine defense

Porcupines are rodents with super defenses! Their bodies have hair, like other mammals, but they also have quills. Quills (a special type of hair) are long, pointy spikes. They are hollow like straws so they're lightweight. On the porcupine's tail are shorter quills. These quills make a noise like a baby rattle. If an animal bothers a porcupine, the porcupine raises all of its quills and rattles its tail quills. If the enemy does not leave, the porcupine charges backward into the intruder. Quills that get stuck into the enemy pull out of the porcupine's fur. Quills are painful so it's best to leave porcupines alone.

Rabbits

Rabbits are furry animals that live in most parts of the world. They even live in the cold areas of North America. Rabbits are herbivores, or planteaters. They use sharp front teeth to nibble grass, twigs, and leaves. Rabbits depend on their eyesight and excellent hearing to escape from animals that want to kill them. If a rabbit senses danger, it thumps the ground with its back feet. This loud sound warns the other rabbits. A rabbit's best defense is to run away. Wild rabbits can be farmland pests. They eat farmers' crops. Some rabbits live underground in burrows. Rabbits have been bred for pets, and today there are about 60 types of domestic rabbits. Hares are close relatives to rabbits. They look similar except they have extra-long ears, and they don't live in burrows.

Black-tailed Jackrabbit The black-tailed jackrabbit lives in the deserts of the United States. Its long ears are used to listen for danger.

Dwarf The smallest rabbits are called "dwarf rabbits." They're about half the size of a wild rabbit.

Angora Angora rabbits have long, fine hair, which gets tangled easily. Pet angora rabbits need to be brushed quite often.

Eastern Cottontail Eastern cottontail is the perfect name for this rabbit. The underside of its tail looks just like a cotton ball.

Dutch

Exotic Mammals

Sloths, anteaters, and armadillos are closely related. They all have small teeth or no teeth at all. Sloths are found in the rain forests of Central and South America. They spend most of their time hanging in the trees. They can even fall asleep hanging upside down! Sloths eat leaves and fruit at night. After a baby sloth is born, it hangs onto its mother's fur. Some sloths look green because of algae that grow in their fur. Anteaters have sharp claws and long tongues for finding food. They also use their claws as weapons. Meanwhile, there are 20 species of armadillos. They look like small armored tanks. Hundreds of small scales cover their skin. Armadillos feed on insects, grubs, berries, bird eggs, and occasionally dead animals. They are excellent diggers, and they live underground in burrows.

Two-toed Sloth Sloths may be slow on land, but they're great swimmers. They are not afraid to cross rivers or swamps to find food.

Nine-banded Armadillo The nine-banded armadillo is the only armadillo found in North America. They are the only armadillos that give birth to four identical babies. When bothered by a predator, only a three-banded armadillo can roll up into a ball.

Giant Anteater The giant anteater has a beautiful bushy tail and strong front arms with claws. Giant anteaters can eat up to 30,000 ants in one day.

Mammals that lay eggs

Most mammals give birth to live young. Three kinds of mammals lay eggs. They are called "monotremes." The platypus, found in Australia and Tasmania, is a rather interesting animal. It has a furry body, a beaverlike tail, four webbed feet, and a rubbery beak. Female platypuses lay two to three eggs every year. They curl their bodies around

spiny anteater

platypus

the eggs until they hatch. The babies are then fed milk just like other mammals. The other species of monotreme is the echidna, which is sometimes called the "spiny anteater." Echidnas lay one to three eggs, which they keep warm in a pouch. When the babies hatch, they stay in the pouch drinking milk for about eight weeks.

Bears

Bears are the largest meateating animals on the planet. They have heavy bodies, powerful jaws, and sharp claws. Bears usually walk at a lumbering pace, but they can run. Bears eat an assortment of foods, including fruit, roots, insects, honey, fish, and meat. In winter, some bears find a safe place to hibernate. Hibernation is a deep sleep that may last for many weeks. Right before hibernation, bears eat a lot. Their bodies change the food they eat into fat. When a bear is hibernating, it lives off of its stored fat. The body functions also slow down to save energy. Female polar bears give birth to their cubs during the hibernation season. They have them in their hibernating ice dens. When spring arrives, mother and cubs leave the den.

Grizzly Bear Grizzly bears are also called brown bears. When a grizzly bear stands on its back feet, it can be taller than 9 feet. Grizzlies are strong enough to drag a horse.

Polar Bear Polar bears are the largest bears in the world. Polar bears are great swimmers. Did you know that a polar bear's skin is black?

Spectacled Bear Spectacled bears are the only bears found in South America. They are named after the white rings around their eyes. Spectacled bears do not hibernate like other bears.

Black Bear Black bears are smaller than brown bears. You can often find them in campgrounds, where they may eat food from the garbage cans.

Sun Bear The world's smallest bear is the sun bear. They live in the forests of southeastern Asia. They have short, glossy black fur often with an orange or white breast mark.

Marvelous Mammals **33**

Weasels

The weasel family includes nearly 70 species, including otters, wolverines, polecats, ferrets, minks, badgers, and skunks. Most have long bodies and short legs. They hunt using sight and smell. Even though weasels are small, they are fierce hunters. They can kill animals larger than themselves. They've even been known to scare other predators from their kill. Weasels like to eat mice, rats, other rodents, fish, and birds' eggs. Weasels are so slim that they can crawl down into the burrows of their prey. Ferrets are relatives of polecats. Some varieties have been tamed and can be kept as pets. Hunters still kill minks and badgers for their fur.

River Otter Otters are carnivores that hunt for animals in the water. Otters have long, thin bodies with waterproof fur. They have webbed skin between their toes to help them swim.

Wolverine Wolverines are known for being very strong and very ferocious. In fact, they have chased bears away from their food!

Black-footed Ferret

Skunk defense

Skunks live in the woods and grasslands of North and South America. They are easy to see with their black fur and white stripes. Skunks are famous for the foul smell they make. The smell is the skunk's way of getting rid of predators such as a lynx. The skunk first warns the predator by thumping its paw on the ground. It then turns around and lifts its back legs and rump into the air. If the predator still doesn't leave, the skunk then squirts a stinky liquid at it. The liquid is made by a special gland near the skunk's tail. The foul smell can last for many days.

Aquatic Mammals

Aquatic mammals are mammals that live in water. Instead of legs and arms, they have fins and flippers, which help them to move smoothly through the water. There are more than 80 species of whales and dolphins. Whales and dolphins look like fish, but they're really mammals. They breathe air, have hair, and feed their young with milk. Each of these animals must come up for air. They breathe through openings on the top of their heads called "blowholes." The largest animal in the world is the blue whale.

Seals and sea lions are carnivores, or meateaters. They spend most of their lives in water. They usually come on land to mate and give birth to their young. They are excellent swimmers and divers because they have powerful flippers. Most seals and sea lions feed on fish. They do not have blowholes. They come to the surface and breathe through their mouths and nostrils.

Bottlenose Dolphin Bottlenose dolphins are highly intelligent mammals. They live in groups called "schools." There can be as many as 100 dolphins in a school.

Blue Whale The blue whale uses a substance called "baleen" to eat. Baleen looks like large feathers and works like a filter. Small fish get trapped in the baleen, and the extra water goes out.

Killer Whale Black-and-white killer whales belong to the dolphin family. They communicate with one another by making whistles, clicks, and creaking sounds.

California Sea Lion Shiny, black California sea lions (below) can move better on land than seals can. They have strong front flippers for holding themselves up. Their back flippers can turn forward and work like feet.

Harbor Seal

Walrus Male and female walruses have long tusks. Tusks are teeth that stick out of the walrus's mouth. Walruses suck up clams whole and spit out the empty shells.

Primates

Primates are mammals that include monkeys, apes, and humans. There are more than 200 species of primates. Most monkeys and apes are found in forests and in warm climates. Monkeys have long arms and legs for moving through branches. They live in family groups called "troops." They feed on plants, bird eggs, small animals, and insects. They have large eyes that face forward. This helps them find food and figure out how far away branches are. Many Central and South American monkeys have long tails that can grip things. A tail that can curl and grab things is called a "prehensile tail."

Apes are different from other monkeys because they are larger and do not have tails. They include gorillas, chimpanzees, and orangutans.

Black Spider Monkey Black spider monkeys are the acrobats of the trees! They can swing through the branches faster than most people can walk! Their tails are strong enough to hang on to branches.

Orangutan Orangutans are the only great apes with bright red fur. Males develop large flaps, or pads, around their faces as they get older. Orangutans spend much of their time in the trees.

Mandrill Mandrills are the heaviest monkeys in the world. Males have brightly colored faces. Their muzzles, or noses, are bright red and blue.

Chimpanzee Chimpanzees can use tools to get food. Chimps will use a thin stick to get ants out of an anthill. They'll even use rocks to crack open nuts.

Lowland Gorilla Unlike monkeys, gorillas do not have tails. Gorillas are the largest primates in the world, weighing up to 500 pounds. Gorillas live in forests in groups of up to 20.

The unique lemurs

Lemurs can be found only on the island of Madagascar off the eastern coast of Africa. Because the forests where lemurs live are being destroyed, lemurs are becoming rare. Most lemurs spend their time high in

Sifaka lemur

the trees. They eat fruit, leaves, insects, and eggs. The mouse lemur is the smallest primate. It's about the size of your hand. The largest lemur is the indri, which is about 4 feet tall. The ring-tailed lemur is unique in that it spends a lot of its time on the ground. It walks on four legs and carries its striped tail upright. Lemurs use their tails to warn other lemurs of danger. Lemur babies hang on to their mothers' fur.

Flying lemurs

When you think of flying animals, you probably think of birds. Did you know that there are flying lemurs? These small mammals don't actually fly—they glide! If you watch these lemurs fly from tree to tree, it looks as if they're wearing a cloak or cape. That's the lemur's flight membrane. The membrane is a stretchy flap of skin that lets the lemur sail through the air. The membrane stretches from their necks, down the sides of their bodies, and all the way to their tails. Flying lemurs can sail for more than 125 meters. That's longer than a football field! Flying lemurs are not members of the primate family but form their own order.

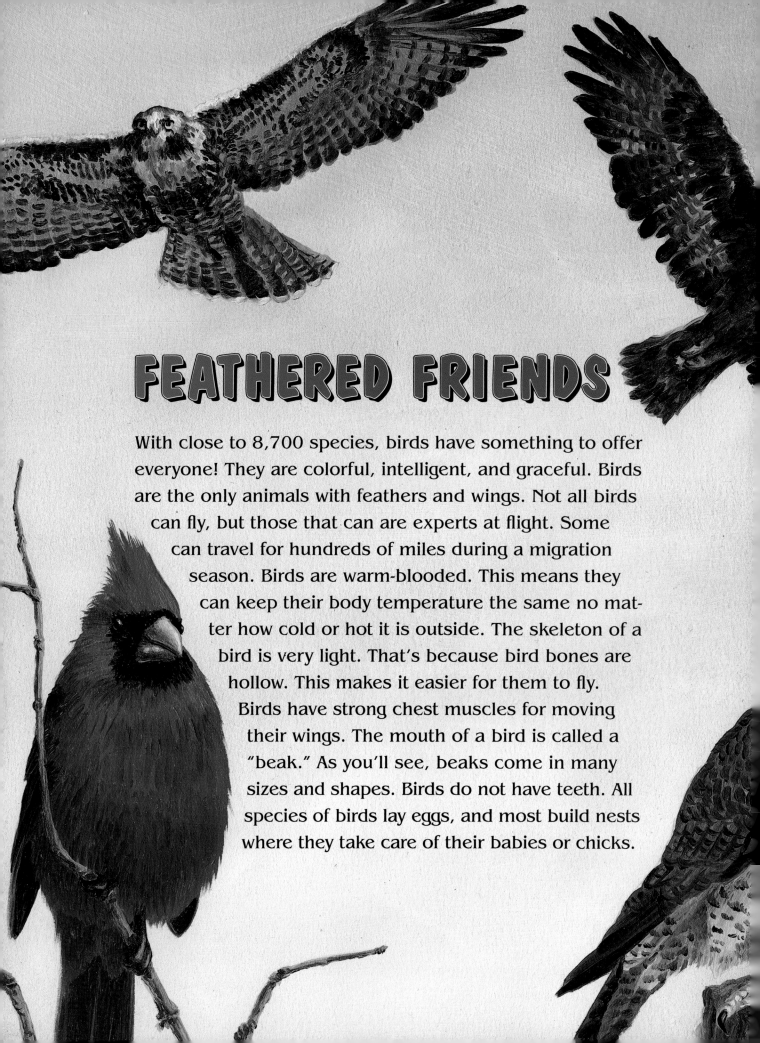

FEATHERED FRIENDS

With close to 8,700 species, birds have something to offer everyone! They are colorful, intelligent, and graceful. Birds are the only animals with feathers and wings. Not all birds can fly, but those that can are experts at flight. Some can travel for hundreds of miles during a migration season. Birds are warm-blooded. This means they can keep their body temperature the same no matter how cold or hot it is outside. The skeleton of a bird is very light. That's because bird bones are hollow. This makes it easier for them to fly. Birds have strong chest muscles for moving their wings. The mouth of a bird is called a "beak." As you'll see, beaks come in many sizes and shapes. Birds do not have teeth. All species of birds lay eggs, and most build nests where they take care of their babies or chicks.

Common North American Birds

North America is a wonderful place to watch birds. As a matter of fact, more than 60 million people do! Bird watching, or birding, is the largest hobby in North America. With more than 900 different bird species, bird watchers can watch the skies for most of their lives. Some North American birds are permanent residents, meaning they live in one area all year long. Some birds stay in one area only for a short time. Then they fly to different places to find food or lay their eggs. You can find birds in snowy places, in forests, by ponds, lakes, or rivers, and even in your backyard.

American Crow This crow has shiny black feathers and a strong beak. Crows sometimes eat animals that are dead on the road. It doesn't sound very tasty, but it's an important job.

Cardinal Male cardinals are bright red and have a crest on their heads. Females are a lighter tan color. They are hard to see when they sit on their nests.

Robin Robins eat worms that they pull from the ground. In the winter, they eat berries and fruit. Male robins have bright red chests and dark heads.

Blue Jay Blue jays are so named because of their color. Their call is very noisy. Blue jays are bold. They scare other birds away from their food and then eat it.

Bird nests

Many animals make nests, but birds are natural nest builders. Just like birds, nests come in a variety of styles. Pigeons make simple nests of sticks and twigs. Orioles weave beautiful nests that hang from the trees. Woodpeckers drill large holes in trees and build their nests inside. If you look inside a tree or fence post, you may find a bluebird nest. Eagles return to the same tree nest every year. Some bird nests are hidden by leaves on the ground. Many birds line the inside of their nest with soft things. Grass, feathers, yarn, paper, and animal hair are just some of the things you may find inside.

Swallow
Swallows catch insects in the air. They make their nests from mud and grass.

Pileated Woodpecker Like all woodpeckers, the pileated woodpecker uses its strong beak to chip away wood. Then it searches for insects inside the tree trunk.

Penguins and Albatrosses

Penguins are seabirds that live in some of the coldest places in the world. They cannot fly, but they are great swimmers. Penguins use their wings as flippers to glide through the water. Penguins can dive when they pull their wings close to their bodies. Their tails and feet are used for steering. Penguins hunt for fish and krill, which is a type of shrimp. Penguins live in large groups called "colonies." When they walk on land, they waddle.

Albatrosses are the largest of all the seabirds. They live in cold southern hemisphere areas. Albatrosses have huge wings and can fly up to 6,000 miles during one trip! Even though their wings are large, they don't flap them often. Instead, they fly close to the ocean's waves and use the wind to glide. When an albatross is hungry, it lands on the water and catches squid. Albatrosses come on land only to raise their young.

Emperor Penguin The largest penguin is the emperor penguin. During the mating season, it's the male that keeps the egg warm. He puts it on top of his feet and covers it with a flap of skin.

Adélie Penguin Adélie penguins live in large, noisy colonies. They make noises to attract a mate or warn the others of danger.

Rockhopper Penguin Rockhopper penguins do just that—they hop! Bushy crests on the top of their heads make them easy to spot. Rockhopper penguins live for about ten years.

Albatross

Large Flightless Birds

Over time, some birds have lost their ability to fly. They are called flightless birds. Flightless birds include such species as the ostrich, cassowary, emu, and rhea. These birds still have wings, but they look different than birds that fly. That's because their wings are used for other things. Ostriches make themselves look bigger to predators by fanning their wings open and shaking them. After the females lay their eggs, males protect the eggs. They use their wings to shade the eggs when it's hot. Ostriches, cassowaries, emus, and rheas have powerful leg muscles. So even though they can't fly, they can run very fast. Ostriches can reach speeds of about 40 miles per hour.

Ostrich The ostrich is the world's largest bird. It's also the only bird that has two-toed feet. Ostriches kick their feet and use their claws against predators.

Rhea

Cassowary Cassowaries are easy to see with their blue and red necks. A large bony plate on their heads, called a "casque," protects them while they run through the woods.

Emu Emus are Australia's tallest birds. Females lay dark green eggs. Males keep the eggs warm until they hatch. Emu babies are born with stripes.

Bird feet

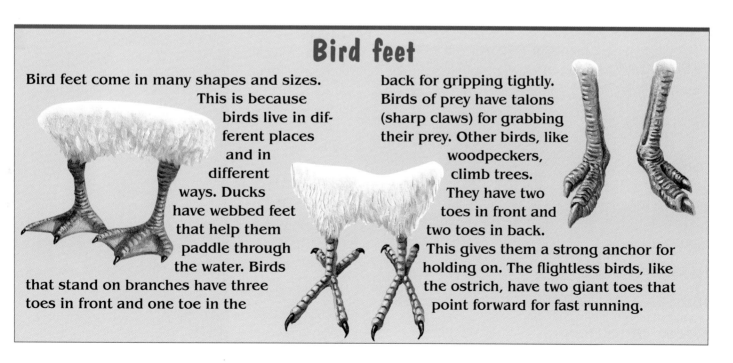

Bird feet come in many shapes and sizes. This is because birds live in different places and in different ways. Ducks have webbed feet that help them paddle through the water. Birds that stand on branches have three toes in front and one toe in the back for gripping tightly. Birds of prey have talons (sharp claws) for grabbing their prey. Other birds, like woodpeckers, climb trees. They have two toes in front and two toes in back. This gives them a strong anchor for holding on. The flightless birds, like the ostrich, have two giant toes that point forward for fast running.

Herons, Storks, Flamingos, and Cranes

These wonderful birds share two main features—long legs and long necks. Most of them live and feed near shallow waters. Some of these birds, like the crane, will watch for fish and then use their sharp beaks to spear them. Others, like the flamingo with its curved beak, filter the water for small plants and animals. Long legs help these birds stand in the water without getting their bodies wet. Their wide toes stop them from sinking in the mud. Long necks help them see fish and other water animals. Unfortunately, many of these birds are becoming rare. Their habitats, or homes, are getting smaller because people are draining water out of the wetlands.

American Flamingos Flamingos often sleep standing on one foot. Female flamingos protect their young chicks by holding them under their wings.

Great Blue Heron

Cattle Egret You can often see cattle egrets standing on the backs of cattle. When the cattle move, they stir up insects in the fields. The egrets then eat the insects.

White Stork Storks are believed to be a sign of good luck. They make nests on rooftops, and they communicate by loudly clapping their beaks open and shut.

Sacred Ibis

Whooping Crane The whooping crane is the tallest bird in North America. It eats many things, including crabs, clams, frogs, and minnows.

Bird beaks

Birds have special shaped beaks that help them eat their favorite foods. Birds that eat insects have small, pointed beaks. Hawks and owls have hooked beaks for tearing apart meat. Woodpeckers eat insects, but they have to find them. They have long, strong beaks to drill into trees where insects hide. Many fish-eating birds, like the heron, have long beaks for stabbing. Hummingbirds have long, hollow beaks for sucking up nectar. Birds that eat hard seeds have short, cone-shaped beaks. Ducks and swans have flat beaks for finding tiny water plants and animals.

Geese and Ducks

Geese, swans, and ducks are known as waterfowl. That's because they spend their lives on or near water. There are more than 150 species of waterfowl. Look at their feet. See how flaps of skin are in-between their toes? These are called "webbed feet." They work like paddles and help the birds move through the water. Waterfowl have waterproof feathers. This keeps the skin underneath dry and warm. Waterfowl have beaks shaped like small shovels. Most get their food from the water. They eat water plants, small fish, or insects. Geese come to land to feed. They pull up grass and other plants with their beaks. Waterfowl lay their eggs in nests that they build on land. Females sit on their eggs to keep them warm. Babies are called "chicks." A few hours after hatching, chicks can swim!

Mute Swan The mute swan is a large, beautiful bird. It uses its long neck to reach for food in the water. Swans reach so far that their bottoms stick up in the air!

Canada Goose Canada geese are brown and white with black heads. They make loud honking sounds as they fly. Canada geese fly in a V-shape when they migrate.

American Wood Duck

Mallards Mallards are found all over the world. Males have bright green heads. Females are brown. They are hard to see when they sit on their nests.

Migration

Some birds live in places where there's food all year round. This is usually where the temperature is warm and food can grow easily. In other areas, the summer and winter seasons are very different. Birds can no longer find enough food to live in the winter so they migrate. Migration is a long journey that animals make to find food or to breed. Canada geese fly to warmer areas in the south to find food. Swallows migrate to raise their babies. Other animals such as whales, antelope, turtles, butterflies, and fish migrate, but birds travel the farthest.

Vultures, Hawks, and Eagles

Vultures, hawks, and eagles are called "birds of prey." They are excellent hunters because of their speed and strength. Except for vultures, birds of prey must find and kill their food. They use their keen eyesight to find their prey. It may be a mouse, a small rabbit, or even another bird. With super speed, they fly after and dive at their prey. Then they use their claws, called talons, to grab it. Birds of prey rip their food apart with their hooked beaks. Since birds don't have teeth, they must rip the pieces small enough to swallow whole. There are about 290 species of birds of prey around the world.

Golden Eagle

Red-tailed Hawk The red-tailed hawk is the most common hawk in North America. They live in woods, open fields, and deserts. They eat rodents.

California Condor California condors are an endangered species. There is only a small number of them left in California and Arizona. Scientists are breeding condors in zoos and then releasing them into the wild.

Vulture

Peregrine Falcon The peregrine falcon is the world's fastest bird. To do a fast dive, the peregrine falcon pulls its wings close to its body.

Our national bird: American bald eagle

The American bald eagle is the national bird of the United States. This bird of prey is not really bald! Its body has brown feathers, but its head has white feathers. This gives the appearance that it is bald. The eagle has been a symbol of power and majesty for thousands of years. Eagles live near rivers, lakes, and ocean coasts. They use strong wings, sharp eyes, and powerful talons to capture food. Eagles eat mostly fish. Their hooked bills are perfect for tearing up their food. Eagles mate for life and return to the same nest every year.

Pheasant, Quail, and Peacocks

Birds that people hunt are called "game birds." They include wild turkey, partridge, pheasant, quail, peacock, and grouse. Game birds have plump bodies and short legs. They spend most of their time on the ground searching for food. They eat seeds, insects, and grubs. Claws help them to scratch the ground and find food. Game birds can fly, but they usually don't go very far. If startled, they run away. Males and females look different from each other. Males have bright colors to attract a mate. Females have plain, dull colors. This camouflages them from predators while they sit on their nests.

Turkey Male turkeys look different than female turkeys. Males are very colorful. They also have flaps of skin hanging from their heads and necks. This is called a "wattle." A female turkey is called a "hen" and does not have a wattle.

Bobwhite

Ring-necked Pheasant The adult male ring-necked pheasant shows how this bird got its name. The green color on its head stops at a bright white ring at the neck.

Red Jungle Fowl Red jungle fowl are early relatives of chickens. They live in India and Asia. The males even make crowing sounds like chickens.

Peafowl Peafowl are also known as peacocks. Male peacocks use their long colorful tail feathers to attract a mate. Females are called "peahens."

Pigeons and Doves

Pigeons are found throughout the world. You can find them in the woods, grasslands, and even in cities. Pigeons and doves have plump bodies and small heads. Their heads move back and forth as they walk. They have small beaks for eating seeds. Pigeons, as well as their relatives (in the *Columbidae* family), can suck water up into their beaks. All other birds must take a mouthful and tilt their heads back to swallow. The females lay two to three eggs at a time. When the chicks hatch, pigeons and doves do something very unusual—they make a milky fluid in their throats and feed it to the chicks.

Rock Dove This gray rock dove is a close relative of street pigeons. Wild rock doves build nests on cliff ledges.

Bird heads

When you look at the birds in the world, you will be amazed at the different types of heads you'll find. Many birds, like seagulls, have heads where the feathers lie flat. The cardinal and kingfisher have a crest, which is a group of feathers that can stick up. The Victoria crowned pigeon has a beautiful set of lacy feathers on top of its head. The great horned owl has two tufts of feathers that look like ears. Not all birds have beautiful, feather-covered heads. The wood stork and turkey vulture have wrinkly, bald heads. Although they're not pretty, their heads stay cleaner when they feed.

Homing pigeons

Pigeons were trained as homing birds during the Egyptian and Roman Empires. Homing pigeons can find their way home over long distances. Warriors would carry pigeons from their homelands as they traveled off to war. They would attach a message to the pigeon's leg and release it. The pigeon would fly home where the message would be read. In times when there were no telephones or computers, they were the fastest way to get information from one place to another. Today, people race pigeons to see which can get home the fastest.

Mourning Dove The mourning dove is named because of the soft, sad cooing sound it makes. Mourning doves always feed in pairs or small flocks.

Exotic Birds
(Parrots, Cockatoos, Macaws, and Parakeets)

These exotic birds have strong, hooked beaks for cracking open nuts, breaking apart fruit, and even pulling themselves up on a branch! Parrots have fat toes and sharp claws. They use them to pick up food and climb through the trees. Exotic birds can make a wide variety of sounds. Some have been trained to say human words. Many of the world's parrots are facing extinction. Deforestation and illegal hunting are making it difficult for these birds to survive.

Scarlet Macaw
Macaws are the world's largest parrots. They have brightly colored feathers. Macaws screech loudly to communicate.

Moluccan Cockatoo Cockatoos are the only parrots that have a crest on their heads. Cockatoos have four toes for gripping. Two toes point forward, and two toes point backward.

African Gray Parrot The African gray parrot is not entirely gray. It has bright red tail feathers. These birds are experts at copying human words.

Parakeet Parakeets are popular pets. They come in many colors, but wild parakeets are always yellow and green.

Types of feathers

Contour

Flight

Flight

Down

Contour

Birds have three types of feathers. *Down* feathers are soft and fluffy. They are right next to the bird's skin and help keep it warm. *Contour* feathers cover most of the bird's body. They can come in many colors and sizes. When you find a feather on the ground, it's usually a contour feather. *Flight* feathers are special forms of contour feathers. You find them on the bird's wing tips and tail. They help the bird to fly.

Owls

Owls are nocturnal birds of prey. This means they hunt for live animals at night. Owls have great eyesight and hearing. They can move their heads almost all the way around, which helps them hear things from various locations. Owls can fly almost silently because they have soft feathers. Owls use their sharp claws, or talons, to catch food. Owls eat mice, rats, and snakes. During the day, owls live in hollow trees and in the old nests left by other large birds, or even in buildings. The burrowing owls are unique in that they live in holes they make in the ground. Owls give birth to fluffy babies called owlets.

Great Horned Owl North America's largest owl is the great horned owl. It is large enough to kill a skunk. It is named for the hornlike tufts of feathers on its head.

Barn Owl Barn owls are found throughout the world. They have flat, heart-shaped faces. Their hearing is so good that they can find their prey in complete darkness.

Snowy Owl The snowy owl lives in the tundra of the Arctic. Its white feathers camouflage it in the snow. Females have black marks in their feathers.

Hummingbirds

When hummingbirds fly, all you hear is a soft humming noise. This is how they got their name. Their wings beat so quickly that you can hardly see them. There are about 320 species of hummingbirds that live in the warm places of North and South America. Hummingbirds have long, thin beaks for getting nectar out of flowers. Nectar is full of sugar, which the hummingbirds need for energy. Hummingbird wings are special because they swivel. They can move up and down, which lets them hover in the air. Hummingbirds can even fly backward!

Ruby-throated Hummingbird The ruby-throated hummingbird is named for the red color under its beak. It beats its wings more than 70 times a second.

Streamer-tail Hummingbird

WET AND WILD SEA CREATURES

Many of the planet's animals cannot be seen by looking out a window. They are hidden in oceans, lakes, rivers, and streams. Some, like shrimp and krill, are quite small. Others, like the whale shark, are as huge as a truck. In this chapter we will look at fish that have skeletons made of cartilage, which is rubbery and can bend easily. Sharks and rays are these types of fish. We'll also look at fish with bony skeletons, like salmon and trout. There's also a section on aquarium fish. These are fish you can buy at a store and keep as pets. The last section is on other special animals found in the water.

Sharks and Rays

Sharks and rays are fish with cartilage skeletons. The end of your nose is made of cartilage! Shark skin is rough, and their fins are stiff. Sharks swim with a side-to-side motion. They use their tails to push themselves through the water. Rays flap their fins like wings. Both sharks and rays have powerful jaws. Sharks like to eat fish, crabs, clams, squid, and whales, as well as other sharks. Rays have flat teeth for crushing clams and oysters. To find a ray's mouth, look underneath its body. Many sharks and rays give birth to live young.

Hammerhead Shark Hammerhead sharks have odd-shaped bodies. Their heads have long flaps that stick out to the sides.

Whale shark

The whale shark is the largest fish in the world. It can weigh more than 15 tons, which is more than 280 people! Its mouth is so big that a small person could lie sideways inside its mouth and still have a little room left over. These gentle creatures are not interested in people or large fish as food. They eat plankton (very small animal and plant life), which live at the surface of the ocean. To eat, whale sharks float along and take big gulps of water. They filter out the plankton in their gills and then get rid of the water.

Leopard Shark Leopard sharks get their name from the dark brown spots on their skin. Leopard sharks swim on the ocean bottom and eat clams and other mollusks.

Young Tiger Shark Tiger sharks will eat just about anything.

Sharks and Rays

Great White Shark The great white shark is the largest predatory shark. An adult can be as long as 23 feet, which is about as long as two cars!

Stingray Stingrays have round bodies with fins that flap like wings. They hide under the sand when they're not swimming. Sometimes, all you can see are their eyes.

Manta Ray The manta ray is the largest ray in the world. It uses large, fleshy horns on the sides of its head to guide food into its mouth underneath its body. Manta rays eat plankton (tiny animal and plant life in the ocean), as well as small fish and little crustaceans, such as shrimps and crabs.

Sharks and remoras

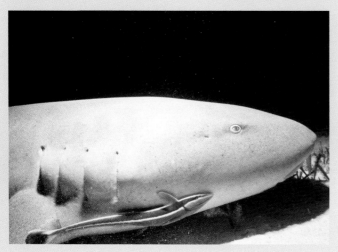

Sometimes you'll see small fish attached to sharks. These fish are remoras, or shark suckers. The remora has a disc-shaped sucker on top of its head. It presses and flattens the sucker to the shark's body. This does not hurt the shark. The remora gets a free ride through the water and eats little pieces of food that the shark misses. Remoras also eat small, harmful animals off of a shark's skin. Remoras will attach to whales and porpoises, too. This type of relationship in which both animals benefit is called "a symbiotic relationship."

Bony Fish

There are more than 24,000 species of bony fish. Bony fish have skeletons made out of bone—just like yours! Their bodies are covered with scales that overlap each other. Scales protect the fish from rough rocks and other fish. Bony fish can live in lakes, rivers, streams, and oceans. They breathe using special body parts called gills, which are hidden behind flaps on the sides of their bodies. The gills are a pinkish color and are stacked like the pages of a book.

Fish come in many colors. Some, like the pike, have patterns that help them hide. Some fish change colors during the mating season. Most bony fish lay their eggs in the water and then leave. The young fish take care of themselves when they're born.

Pacific Salmon

Rainbow Trout Rainbow trout are popular with anglers. They are originally from North America but have been introduced to lakes throughout the world.

American Bullhead

Chinook The chinook is the largest of the Pacific salmon. Most weigh about 20 pounds. The record for the largest chinook is 126 pounds.

Glass Catfish You can clearly see where this fish got its name! Like many fish, glass catfish live in groups called "schools."

Mudskipper

The mudskipper is a unique fish. It lives in swamps and on muddy coasts. When the water level is high, it hides in its burrow. When the water level is low, it skips across the mud on its front fins. Mudskippers can even climb up tree roots! Look closely at their front fins and see how muscular they are. This gives them strength to move outside of water. Mudskippers use their gills to breathe underwater. On land, they breathe through their skin. Mudskippers can survive for hours out of the water, but they must keep their skin wet.

Eels

With their long, thin, wiggly bodies, you might think that eels are snakes. Well, they're not—they're fish! Most eels don't have scales like other fish. Their bodies are smooth and slippery. Eels have a ribbonlike fin that runs down their backs, around their tails, and underneath their bodies. They move like snakes in the water. There are more than 500 species of eel living in fresh and salt water throughout the world. Adult female eels lay eggs but don't take care of them. When the eggs hatch, the babies drift along in the water's current. Baby eels are called "elvers." Some eels migrate thousands of miles to breed and lay their eggs. Many go back to the place where they were born.

Electric Eel Electric eels use special cells in their tails to make an electric shock. The shock is strong enough to knock a human out!

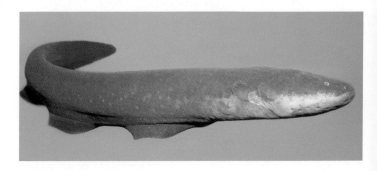

Moray Eel Moray eels are brightly colored. They spend most of their lives hidden under rocks or in coral. They grab food as it goes by.

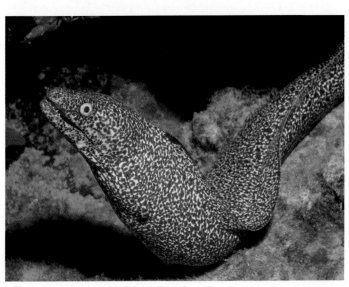

Protection

Animals must have a way to protect themselves from predators. Besides hiding by camouflage or using an electric shock like the eel, some sea creatures find other ways to defend themselves. The lionfish is beautiful with its stripes and feathery fins, but look out! At the ends of its fins are sharp spines that can inject a strong poison. Stingrays have one or two stingers at the base of their tail. They also inject poison if a predator attacks.

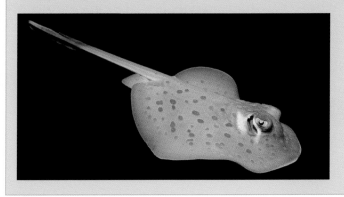

Deep-Water Fish

Because these fish live deep in the ocean, they are rarely seen. These deep-water fish share two features. Many have hinged teeth. Some, like the viperfish, have teeth so large they don't even fit in their mouths! Another interesting feature is that they have special organs on their bodies that make light. Light made by living things is called "bioluminescence." One species, called "the triplewart sea devil," has a long strand above its head. The fish lights the end of the strand and dangles it in front of its mouth. Smaller fish are attracted to it, and—GULP—they get eaten in one swallow.

Viperfish Viperfish are not the prettiest animals in the world. They have long, needlelike teeth and big eyes. Their bodies are covered in a slimy jelly.

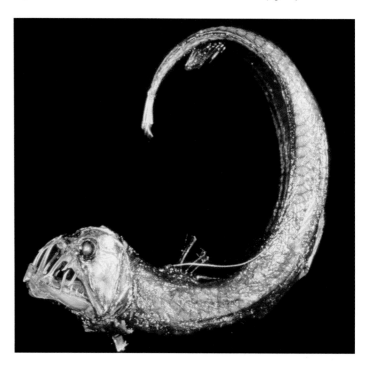

Hatchet Fish Hatchet fish get their name from the shape of their bodies. Schools of hatchet fish use their lights to keep in touch with one another.

Tuna, Mackerel, and Billfish

Some of the larger bony fish in the ocean are tuna, mackerel, and other species of billfish. Tuna have rather thick bodies and a variety of colors in their scales. Tuna have a special organ called a "swimbladder." It's a sac that can be filled with gas. When it's full, the fish floats. When it's empty, it sinks. Tuna also live in schools. Mackerel are long, skinny fish. They have shiny blue and green stripes that camouflage, or hide, them in the water. Billfish include marlins, sailfish, spearfish, and swordfish. All species of billfish are found in warm ocean waters. Swordfish have also been seen in the North Atlantic. They have a long upper jaw, which is shaped like a sword. Most have a fanlike fin on their backs. The sailfish has the largest fin and is the fastest of the billfish. These species hunt small fish and can weigh up to 2,000 pounds.

Bluefin Tuna Bluefin tuna can become extremely large. An adult bluefin tuna can weigh over 1,000 pounds!

Yellowfin Tuna

Mackerel Mackerel have slender bodies. They can swim faster when they flatten their fins to their bodies. Mackerel migrate to warmer waters to breed.

Marlin The marlin is found in warm seas throughout the world. It has a pointy snout that slashes through schools of fish. The stunned fish are then swallowed.

Swordfish The swordfish looks like a marlin except for its snout. The swordfish has a flattened snout like a sword. It is a purple-blue color.

Master hunter: The barracuda

The barracuda is a dangerous sea predator. It has a torpedo-shaped body that makes it very quick in the water. Its mouth has a lower jaw that sticks out and sharp, dagger-like teeth. It can rip through the flesh of other fish quickly and easily. What makes the barracuda an even greater hunter is that it hunts in groups, or packs. These fish have been known to attack divers, especially if they are carrying shiny objects that look like fish.

Wet and Wild Sea Creatures **73**

Fishes of the Reef

Fish that live near coral reefs are some of the most beautiful fish in the world. They also have some of the cleverest ways to survive. Triggerfish and puffer species come in a variety of colors and patterns, though their body shape doesn't vary much at all. They all have small mouths and unusual teeth. How do these fairly small fish protect themselves? Well, the puffer fish will swallow lots of water and swell up like a balloon! This makes them difficult to eat so most predators leave them alone. The triggerfish can lodge itself in the coral reef. Parrotfish get their name from their teeth. They are joined together and look like a bird's beak. They use them to bite pieces of the reef. They chew so loudly that you can hear them underwater! Wrasse fish are small reef fish that usually swim with the larger fish of the reef (read caption to the right).

Queen Triggerfish The queen triggerfish has beautiful colors and very sharp teeth. They like to eat starfish and sea urchins.

Cleaner Wrasse The cleaner wrasse eats parasites and damaged tissue off other fish. Fish will even hold their mouths open so the wrasse can clean inside!

Protection: Clownfish

The clownfish is not a large fish, so when it comes to protecting itself, it uses another animal as a type of body guard! Sea anemones are reef animals with long, stinging tentacles. The clownfish uses this to its advantage. It has special chemicals in its skin that keep it from being stung. The clownfish can feed right inside the sea anemone and never get hurt. If the clownfish is in danger, it will hide deep within the anemone. Animals will not go after it because they don't want to get stung by the sea anemone.

Puffer Fish

Camouflage

Camouflage is an animal's coloring or covering on its body parts that allows it to match its surroundings. They use it to hide from predators or to surprise their prey. Look closely at this picture. Do you see a fish? It's probably very difficult to see the scorpion fish, which is lying on the rock. The scorpion fish is colored like sand and rock. It is also bumpy like coral. Underwater divers often mistake these fish for parts of the reef. This is a great example of camouflage.

Parrotfish Parrotfish sleep at night. To protect themselves, they wrap themselves up in a bag of mucus. The mucus tastes so bad that enemies don't bother them.

Aquarium Fish

Aquariums, or tanks, were originally used to store fish that were to be eaten. It is believed that the ancient Egyptians and Sumerians were among the first to keep fish for a hobby. Today, you can keep a variety of fish as pets. You can have tropical and coldwater species from both freshwater and marine waters. There are many things to consider when putting together an aquarium. First, you need to think about the types of fish you'd like to have. Will some grow too big for the tank? Do certain fish like living in schools? If fish come from different parts of the world, will they get along? It is always best to learn as much as you can before starting an aquarium. That way, both you and your fish will be happy!

Angelfish Angelfish look like thin triangles with long fins. They come in a variety of colors and patterns.

Neon Tetra Neon tetras have slim bodies with electric blue-green stripes. Their fins are almost clear. Neon tetras are peaceful fish and do well in large groups.

Goldfish Goldfish are some of the most popular aquarium fish. They come in many shapes and sizes, like the bubble-eye goldfish. Goldfish can have a single tail fin or a double.

Beta Beta fish have thick bodies, long fins under their bellies, and a fat tail fin. Males can be territorial and tend to fight.

Tiger Barb The tiger barb fish has a pale brown body and dark black stripes. They tend to bite off the fins of other fish so they should not be mixed with angelfish.

Other Aquatic Creatures

The sea is home to a wide assortment of animals. Some are very slow moving, like the starfish. Others prefer not to move much at all, like seahorses and clams. Crabs and lobsters have hard shells and big pincers to protect themselves. Other creatures, like the octopus, are squishy and slimy. Still other animals are able to benefit from living close to the sea. Crabs, for example, spend part of their time in the water and part of their time on land. No matter what type of animal, each has found a successful way to survive in the ocean.

Seahorse Seahorses are beautiful animals but poor swimmers. They hide in water weeds and hang on with their tails. Male seahorses carry the eggs and give birth to the young.

Clam Clams have soft bodies protected inside two shells. They breathe and eat using a pair of siphons. One brings in water and food while the other gets rid of waste.

Octopus An octopus has eight legs covered with suction cups. Female octopuses guard their eggs in a lair and die after they hatch.

Coelacanth

The coelacanth is a large, primitive fish that first appeared more than 350 million years ago. Scientists thought it was extinct until one was caught off the coast of South Africa in 1938. It is believed the coelacanth is the closest living relative of the first fish that came ashore to live on land. This led to the development of other animals like amphibians, reptiles, birds, and mammals.

Other Aquatic Creatures

Crab There are more than 4,000 types of crabs. They have pincers used for grabbing things. Most crabs live near water.

Starfish There are about 2,000 different types of starfish. They can have from 5 to 50 arms. Starfish eat by crawling over their food and pulling it open with their arms.

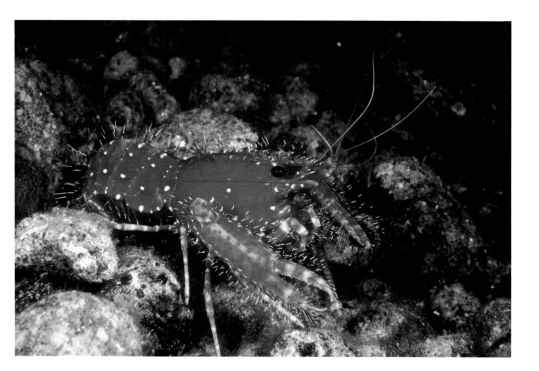

Lobster Lobsters have eight small legs and two large ones. They use their front claws to crack open shells and tear apart small fish. Females carry their eggs under their tails.

Piranha

There are more than 50 species of piranha. They live in the rivers of South America. Some eat fruit that falls into the river, but others are fierce predators. Piranhas have

blunt faces and a lower jaw that sticks out. Inside their mouths are tiny, sharp teeth. This mouth shape is perfect for biting off chunks of meat from other animals. Piranhas live in schools and normally eat other river fish. If an animal gets into the water, piranhas attack in a deadly feeding frenzy. They rip the flesh off of an animal in a matter of seconds!

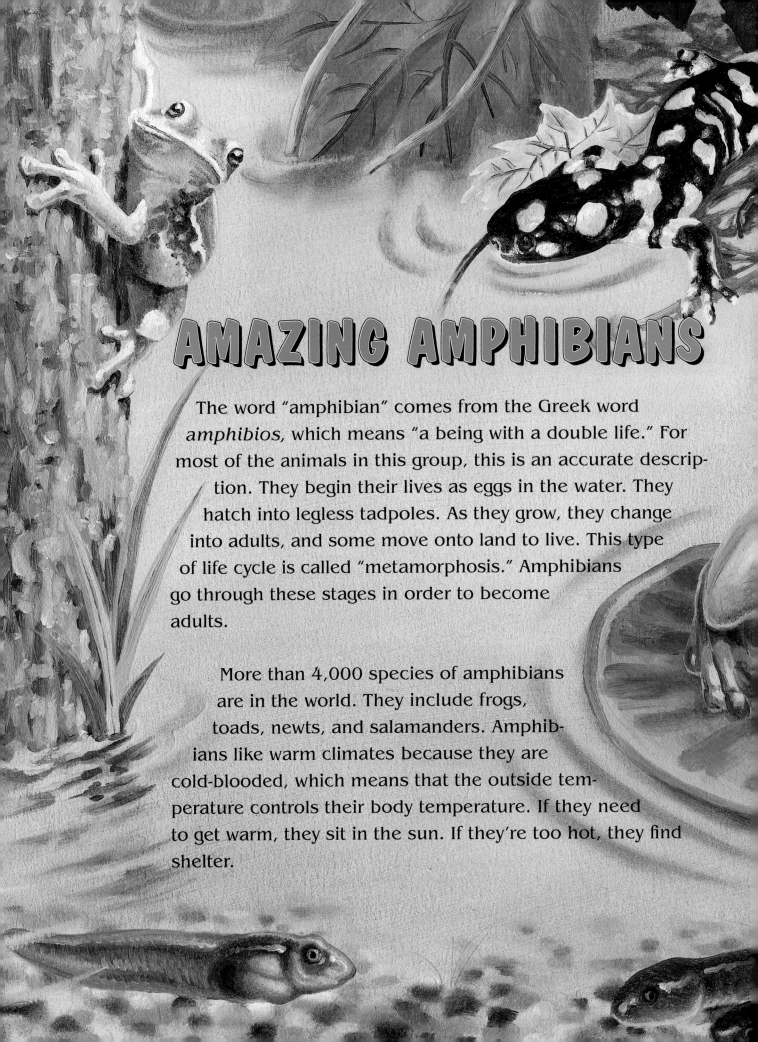

AMAZING AMPHIBIANS

The word "amphibian" comes from the Greek word *amphibios*, which means "a being with a double life." For most of the animals in this group, this is an accurate description. They begin their lives as eggs in the water. They hatch into legless tadpoles. As they grow, they change into adults, and some move onto land to live. This type of life cycle is called "metamorphosis." Amphibians go through these stages in order to become adults.

More than 4,000 species of amphibians are in the world. They include frogs, toads, newts, and salamanders. Amphibians like warm climates because they are cold-blooded, which means that the outside temperature controls their body temperature. If they need to get warm, they sit in the sun. If they're too hot, they find shelter.

Salamanders and Newts

Salamanders and newts look like wet lizards. Although salamanders have short bodies and newts have long bodies, they all have a tail. Most have four legs and smooth, flexible skin. They do not have scales. Salamanders and newts live in the moist, wooded areas of Europe, Asia, North Africa, and North America. Many salamanders and newts can breathe through their skin, which needs constant moisture. Both are carnivorous, eating animals such as insects, slugs, snails, and worms.

Salamanders and newts hatch from jellylike eggs. They go through many changes before becoming adults. When they are born, they are called "tadpoles." They have a tail and feathery gills for breathing. As they grow, they develop legs, and some never lose their gills.

Mudpuppy Mudpuppies keep their feathery gills as they grow into adults. They are nocturnal animals, meaning they are active at night. Females lay 30 to 190 eggs per year.

Texas Blind Salamander The Texas blind salamander is ghostly white. It has red, feathery gills and long, thin legs. Its eyes don't work. They're just black dots buried under the skin.

Eastern Newt
During the mating season, male Eastern newts attract females with their spots. They also call attention to themselves by fanning their tails and by wiggling.

Tiger Salamander
Many salamanders make poison in their skin. Salamanders will warn predators of this poison by having bright colors or patterns on their skin. It's their way of saying, "Back off!"

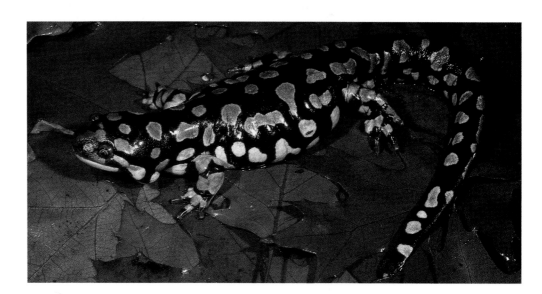

Giant salamander

There are three species of giant salamanders. They all live in rivers and large streams. Giant salamanders never leave the water and spend most of their time beneath rocks. Their skin colors hide them well. This is called "camouflage." Although they are large and rather ugly, they are harmless to people. They feed on fish, worms, insects, crayfish, and snails. They feed mostly at night and rely on smell and touch to find their prey. They have poor eyesight. Giant salamanders can grow as long as five feet. Their skin makes a toxic slime that keeps predators away.

Frogs and Toads

Frogs and toads make up the largest group of amphibians. Most people recognize them by their short bodies and powerful back legs. Their back feet have flaps of skin between the toes. This helps them swim and hop. Frogs and toads have loud calls. They use these sounds to attract a mate during the breeding season. Frogs and toads are cold-blooded, which means that their bodies stay at the same temperature as the outside temperature. Most will avoid the hot sun by burrowing in the mud or hunting for food at night. Frogs and toads eat insects, slugs, and worms. They capture them with long, sticky tongues. You may wonder how frogs and toads are different. Toads normally move by crawling and spend their lives on land. Frogs move by hopping and can live either in water or on land near wet places.

American Toad The American toad is a common visitor in gardens and backyards. It's helpful because it eats garden pests like insects and slugs. Females can lay up to 8,000 eggs.

American Bullfrog Bullfrogs are the largest frogs in North America. They eat anything they can swallow, including turtles, rats, and even bats. Males have vocal sacs under their chins.

Life cycle of frogs and toads

Frogs and toads have similar life cycles. A life cycle is the process an animal goes through to grow up: (1) Females lay eggs, called "spawn," in the water; (2) in two weeks, tadpoles hatch. They have round bodies, long tails, and no legs. Tadpoles breathe through gills; (3) in a few weeks, tadpoles grow hind legs; (4) next, the tadpoles grow front legs. They now look like small frogs or toads but with tails; (5) soon after, their gills shrink, their tails get shorter, and they develop lungs; (6) the small adult is now ready to live on land.

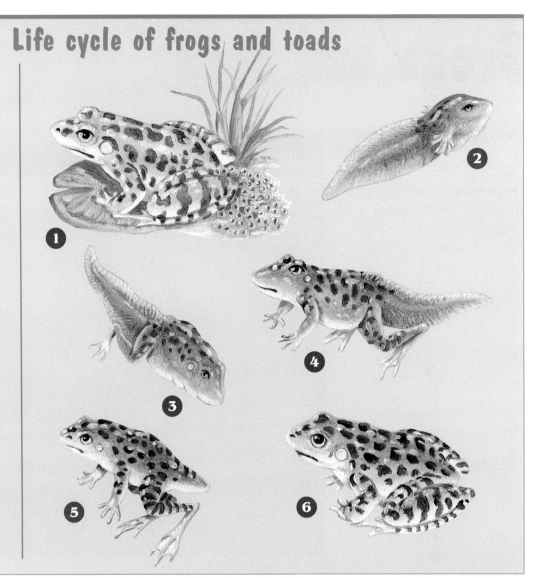

Poison arrow frogs

All frogs and toads make poison from special glands in their skin, but most are not harmful to humans. Poison arrow frogs make some of the most toxic poisons in the world! These species are found in Central and South America. Most poison arrow frogs are brightly colored. This is to warn predators, like birds, to stay away. Some human tribes use the frog's poison for hunting. They dip their arrows in it and hunt for deer, monkeys, and birds. The toxin from one frog is strong enough to make 50 hunting arrows. That's how these peculiar frogs got their name.

Frogs and Toads

Dainty Green Tree Frog Notice the toes on this dainty green tree frog. They are perfect for gripping the tropical plants where they live. Males use large vocal sacs to make a "waaaaaa" sound.

Catching prey: Frogs

Frogs have large eyes for finding food. Depending on the species, frogs eat other frogs, insects, snakes, slugs, or even small mammals. Frogs are carnivores, which means they eat meat. They have a padlike tongue that is attached to the front of their mouths. This lets them flip their tongues out at their food. The top of the tongue pad is sticky. When it lands on the prey, the prey gets stuck or trapped. The frog brings its tongue back into its mouth with the food attached. It's like bringing in a fish on a fishing line.

SCALY SPECIES

Reptiles are animals with tough, scaly skin. Reptiles
include alligators, crocodiles, turtles, lizards, and snakes.
There are about 6,000 species of reptiles found on land
and in the water. They live in most parts of the world,
except where it gets really cold. This is because reptiles
are cold-blooded, which means that their bodies stay at
the same temperature as the outside temperature. Reptiles must warm themselves by lying in the sun. When they
are too hot, they must move into the shade. Snakes and
lizards use their tongues to sense or taste chemicals in
the air, which can lead them to their prey. Most reptiles lay
waterproof eggs. Turtles and crocodiles lay eggs that are
hard. Snakes and lizards lay eggs that are soft and feel
like leather. A few reptiles give birth to live young. Many
people think reptiles are slimy, but they're not. The
scales that protect their skin are shiny and dry.
Most reptiles shed their skin as they grow.

Alligators and Crocodiles

There are more than 20 species of alligators and crocodiles. They are the largest reptiles alive today. All species live in or near water. Their habitats include swamps, lakes, and rivers. They have strong claws and jaws with sharp teeth. Their long tails can be used for protection. Crocodiles and alligators are hard to see when they're in the water. Only their eyes and nostrils show above the water's surface. This helps them surprise their prey. Alligators and crocodiles eat small animals, such as fish and turtles. They can also eat prey as large as zebra or water buffalo. Both alligators and crocodiles lay eggs. Females make nests on land. Some nests are mounds of sand and leaves while other nests are just dips in the ground. Females can lay up to 90 eggs, and they guard them fiercely.

Differences between the alligator and crocodile

It may not seem easy to tell an alligator from a crocodile, but there are certain things to look for. For example, alligators have rounded, U-shaped snouts, or noses. Crocodiles have pointy, V-shaped snouts. The next thing to look at is their mouths. The alligator's upper jaw overlaps its lower jaw. When the alligator's mouth is closed, all you can see are its top jaw teeth. Crocodiles' jaws fit together differently. When their mouths are closed, both the top and bottom jaw teeth show. The fourth upper tooth is especially easy to see.

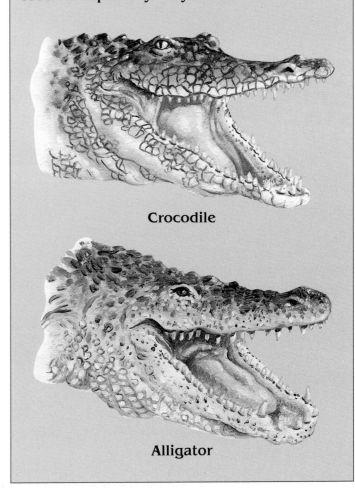

Crocodile

Alligator

American Alligator When baby alligators hatch, they call out to their mother. She picks them up gently in her mouth and carries them into the water.

Nile Crocodile Nile crocodiles prey on animals that come to drink at the river. They drag the animal underwater and drown it. Crocodiles twist their victim's bodies to rip their food apart.

African Dwarf Crocodile

The African dwarf crocodile is the smallest and least-known crocodile. It lives in rainforest rivers and swamps. It climbs on top of fallen tree trunks to bask in the sun.

Scaly Species **93**

Turtles and Sea Turtles

Turtles and tortoises (see next section) are the only reptiles with hard shells. The shell is a great protective feature. The shell is made of two parts: The curved part that protects the back is called the "carapace" while the flat part that protects the underside is the "plastron." The shell is made of solid bone and is covered by thin scales called "scutes." Most turtles can pull their heads inside their shells. A few can pull their legs and tail inside as well. The rest of the turtle's body is also covered by scales. Meanwhile, sea turtles spend their entire lives in water, but they do not have scales. Instead, they have a flexible, leather-like skin. The legs of sea turtles are shaped like flippers. They flap their front flippers and swim through the water. Turtles and tortoises reproduce by laying eggs, which are usually buried underground.

Alligator snapping turtle

The alligator snapping turtle is the largest and most dangerous freshwater turtle. It has a bumpy shell, spiky neck, and power-ful, razor-sharp jaws. The snapper lies qui-etly at the bottom of a lake or river with its mouth open. It lures food to it using its tongue. The turtle wiggles a pink, wormlike piece of skin on the end of its tongue. Pass-ing fish think it's food and enter the turtle's mouth. The turtle snaps its jaws shut and enjoys a meal. Alligator snapping turtles also eat frogs, snakes, and crayfish.

Common Snapping Turtle (above) Snap-ping turtles protect themselves by quickly snapping or biting at things. Why don't they just hide in their shells? They can't—they're too big!

Painted Turtle (below) The painted turtle gets its name from its colorful shell. It lives in ponds, marshes, lakes, and slow-moving rivers. Many species of painted turtles are endangered.

Soft-Shelled Turtle Soft-shelled turtles have just that— soft shells! The shell is usually round and flat. They have long noses for snorkeling and sniffing in cracks for food.

Green Turtle Green turtles spend almost their entire lives at sea. They feed on seaweed by nipping off pieces with their sharp-edged jaws. Females lay about 100 eggs during the breeding season.

Sea turtles and egg laying

The only time a female sea turtle comes onto land is to lay her eggs. During the night, she uses her flippers to pull herself across the beach. She then uses her back flippers to dig a deep hole. About 100 soft-shelled eggs are then put into the hole. The female uses her back flippers to cover the eggs. After a short rest, she returns to the sea. In about three months, the babies hatch from the eggs. They quickly dig their way out of the nest and head for the sea. Many of them are eaten by birds and other predators.

Young Leatherback Turtle When fully grown, the leatherback is the world's largest turtle. Its shell feels rubbery and does not have scales. It feeds on jellyfish and can dive almost one mile underwater.

Tortoises

Tortoises are different than turtles in that they live on land. Both have a protective shell made up of the carapace and plastron. Tortoises are also covered by scales called "scutes." Tortoises are slow-moving land animals. Many can protect themselves by pulling their heads, feet, and tails into their shells. Tortoises can be found in Africa, Asia, Australia, Europe, and North and South America. Tortoises grow slowly and can live to be more than 150 years old! Tortoises do not have teeth. They are herbivores, which means they eat plants. Tortoises use a tough, horny "beak" on their top jaw to rip off pieces of food. The pieces are usually swallowed whole. Females lay their eggs in sandy nests. They cover them with soil and let the heat of the sun incubate them. After several months, the eggs hatch and the babies dig their way to the surface.

Gopher Tortoise The gopher tortoise is so named because it digs burrows like a gopher. The burrow is a long tunnel with a large chamber at the end.

Madagascar Radiated Tortoise The Madagascar radiated tortoise is one of the rarest in the world. The endangered species laws protect it, but people still hunt it for food.

Lizards

Lizards make up over half of the world's reptiles. Most of them live in warm places. This is because they are cold-blooded and need the heat to warm themselves. Many lizards have skin that will turn darker in the sun. This helps them absorb more heat. Most lizards live on the ground and are active during the day. Lizards have long bodies, long legs, and long tails. Their long legs allow them to move very quickly. Lizards that live in trees have claws at the ends of their feet. This helps them grasp branches. Lizards have dry scaly skin. They have good eyesight, which they use to hunt insects. Lizards do not have eyelids. They keep their eyes clean by licking them. Some lizards have bright patterns to warn predators that they are dangerous. As lizards grow, many of them shed their skin.

Common Iguana The common iguana is one of the world's largest plant-eating lizards. They are difficult to see in the trees. Their green skin camouflages them well in the leaves.

Green Anole Green anoles are found in North and South America while brown anoles live only in South America. They have toes with rounded pads and sharp claws for gripping branches. Green anoles are also called "American chameleons."

Lizards

Horned Lizard The horned lizard protects itself with horns and spines on its body. It can also squirt blood from its eyes. Horned lizards are also called "horned toads."

Komodo dragons

Komodo dragons are not really dragons, but they are the world's largest lizards. Komodo dragons are carnivores, or meateaters. They live on the Indonesian islands about 200 miles south of Bali and eat carrion, which is rotting meat. They also hunt deer and wild pigs. Komodo dragons use their long, forked tongues to taste the air. This taste leads them to dead animals or prey. Komodo dragons can run quickly and are strong enough to bring down a horse. They use their powerful jaws to rip their food to pieces. Komodo dragons can live to be more than 40 years old, but their average age is 20 years old.

Lizards with regenerating tails

Some species of lizards have developed an interesting survival trick. They are able to lose their tails when a predator attacks them. In fact, these lizards will wiggle their tails to get the predator's attention while in serious danger. The predator grabs the lizard's tail, and the lizard immediately breaks it off. The lost tail continues to wiggle and distracts the predator as the lizard gets away. The amazing thing is that most of these lizards can grow a new tail! It's never exactly the same as the original, but it still helps in running, swimming, balancing, mating, and camouflaging.

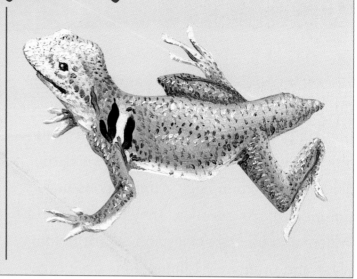

Marine Iguana The marine iguana is the only lizard that lives in the sea. It feeds on seaweed around the Galapagos Islands. It survives the cold waters by slowing its heart rate.

Gila monster

The Gila monster sounds like something out of a scary movie, but it's really a lizard. It lives in the deserts of North America. Its thick body has bright red and black stripes. These colors serve as a warning to predators because the Gila monster has a poisonous bite. Gila monsters eat small mammals, lizards, and frogs. They are most active at dusk when it is cooler. While hunting, the Gila monster grips its prey in its mouth and injects venom as it chews. They do not have fangs but use skinny grooves in their teeth to inject the poison.

Chameleons and Geckos

More than 100 species of chameleons are in the world. About half of these species live on the island of Madagascar. Chameleons usually live in trees but may come down to the ground to lay their eggs. Chameleons have humped, narrow bodies. They have pincerlike fingers and toes specially shaped for holding twigs and branches. Chameleons have eyes that can move separately. One eye can swivel forward while the other is looking backward! Chameleons are special lizards because they can change colors. They do this to match their surroundings, to show their mood, or to correspond to changes in light or temperature levels. Chameleons can do this because of special skin cells called "melanophores." Melanophores change color because of different chemicals in the chameleon's body.

Climbing geckos

Geckos are famous for their climbing abilities. They can climb walls, hang on glass, and even scurry across ceilings. Geckos can do this because of their specially designed feet. If you look at their toes, you will see that they are shaped as fat pads. Each of these pads is divided into overlapping scales. Hundreds of microscopic, hooklike hairs can catch the smallest part of any surface.

Common Chameleon Chameleons have a prehensile tail. That's a tail that can wrap around objects for an extra grip. Chameleons also use their tails for balance.

Jackson's Chameleon The male Jackson's chameleon has three long, pointed horns on its head. These horns are used to attract a mate and fight other males.

How chameleons hunt

Chameleons eat insects and spiders. They sit perfectly still when hunting and move their eyes in different directions in search for food. When prey is spotted, both eyes focus on it. Chameleons sway forward and backward to get a better look and to figure out how far away the prey is. Suddenly, they shoot out their tongue. A chameleon's tongue is two and a half times as long as its body. It has a fat, sticky end, which traps the prey. Just as quickly as it was shot out, the tongue and prey are flicked back into the chameleon's mouth.

Cobras and Coral Snakes

Snakes are one of the most feared and mis-understood animal groups. They are beautiful reptiles that don't have arms or legs. Scales cover their long bodies. People often think they're wet and slimy, but they're not. Their skin is dry and very smooth. Snakes shed their skin as they grow.

Cobras are poisonous snakes found in Africa, India, and Asia. They are often recognized by their flared necks, or hoods. When threat-ened, cobras raise their heads up and spread out their ribs to form a hood. Cobras eat mice, frogs, small mammals, and other snakes. They kill their prey by biting it and injecting venom, or poison, into it.

There are about 40 species of coral snakes. They are small snakes that can be found under leaves and logs. They are nocturnal, which means they hunt at night.

Spitting Cobra Some cobras defend them-selves by spitting venom at their predators' eyes. The venom is extremely painful and can cause permanent blindness. Cobras can spit venom as far as nine feet.

King Cobra King cobras are the largest venomous snakes in the world (up to 18 feet long). Females are unique among snakes because they make nests and sit on top of their eggs.

The king snake's mimicry of the coral snake

The coral snake is a poisonous snake found in the southern United States. Its bright colors warn predators to stay away. Now, look at the nonpoisonous scarlet king snake. Its color pattern is almost the same! This defense is called "mimicry." It's when one animal mimics or copies another animal in the hope that predators will also leave it alone. Look closely though. The coral snake's nose is black. The scarlet king snake's nose is red. The color pattern is also different. Coral snakes have red and yellow bands touching. King snakes do not have red and yellow bands touching.

King snake

Coral snake

Eastern Coral Snake The eastern coral snake has a slender body. It often hunts for prey by slithering down burrow holes. Its bright colors warn predators of its poisonous bite.

Rattlesnakes

Just like other snakes, rattlesnakes do not have teeth for chewing. They do have fangs for injecting venom, but they must swallow their food whole. The bones of their jaws can be unhinged, which allows them to swallow larger animals. Rattlesnakes have an excellent sense of smell; they smell by flicking their tongues in the air. This lets them "taste" scents. They also have special body parts, called "pits," on their snouts. These small holes sense the heat of passing animals. Rattlesnakes use colors and patterns on their skin to camouflage themselves. This allows them to surprise their prey. Rattlesnakes are unique in that they have rattles at the end of their tails. The rattle is made of several loose, bony rings that make a buzzing sound when the tail wiggles. Rattlesnakes use the sound to warn predators or to distract their prey.

Pigmy Rattlesnake The pigmy rattlesnake is only 15–21 inches long. Its rattle is so small that it makes just a soft buzzing noise. It can only be heard from a few feet away.

Eastern Diamondback Rattlesnake
The eastern diamondback rattlesnake is one of the few snakes that give birth to live young. Most snakes lay eggs.

Timber Rattlesnake

Sidewinder Rattlesnake

Sidewinders live in sandy places. Instead of slithering forward, they move sideways across the sand. Horns fold down to protect the snake's eyes when it moves through its underground burrow.

Rattlesnake fangs

Rattlesnakes have large, curved fangs for hunting prey. The fangs can fold away into the snake's jaw when not in use. Fangs are hollow and have a hole at their tips. They are connected to venom sacs that make the poison. When a rattlesnake strikes, it opens its mouth wide, pushes out its fangs, and makes a quick stabbing motion at the animal. The venom sac squeezes the venom through the hollow fangs and into the animal. Rattlesnakes do not use their fangs to hold onto their prey. They bite and then follow the bitten animal until it dies.

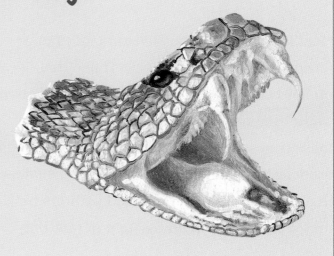

Sea Snakes, Boas, and Pythons

There are about 50 species of sea snakes. Their bodies are shaped differently than other snakes. Their tails are flat and work like paddles. Sea snakes look like ribbons when they swim through the water. Sea snakes have lungs for breathing and must come to the ocean's surface to get fresh air. The lungs help the snake float. When the snake has lots of air in its lungs, it floats. When there is less air in its lungs, it sinks. Sea snakes have nostrils that close when they dive. Some species can dive as deep as 500 feet below the surface. Sea snakes eat fish and eels. They search through rocks and crevices to find their prey, and then they bite it with fangs. The fangs inject poisonous venom that causes the prey to be paralyzed, or unable to move. The prey is then swallowed whole.

Most boas and pythons live on land, but a few can slither up into trees. Those that live on land can be found in dry areas, or even in water. Boas and pythons have prehensile tails. They can be used to grip such things as branches. This is important for those snakes that hunt from trees. Boas and pythons pull their heads back in an S-shape before they

Yellow-bellied Sea Snake Yellow-bellied sea snakes are sometimes found in large schools, just like fish. They give birth to live young.

Black-banded Sea Krait

strike at their prey. They have long teeth that are curved backward into their mouths. Boas and pythons don't kill their prey with venom. They suffocate animals like rodents, birds, bats, and lizards by squeezing them. Once the prey is dead, it is swallowed whole. Extremely large snakes can eat antelope and caiman (a species of alligator). Boas give birth to live young in litters of as many as 50 newborns. Pythons lay eggs.

Giant Anaconda This olive-green anaconda spends its life in or near water feeding on animals that come to drink. It is one of the world's largest and heaviest snakes.

Reticulated Python Reticulated pythons are the longest snakes in the world and can reach ten yards in length. They have pits on their noses for sensing the heat of their prey.

Emerald Boa The beautiful emerald boa is found in rainforest trees. It squeezes and eats its food while hanging by its tail. When done, it pulls itself back up into the trees.

Boa Constrictor

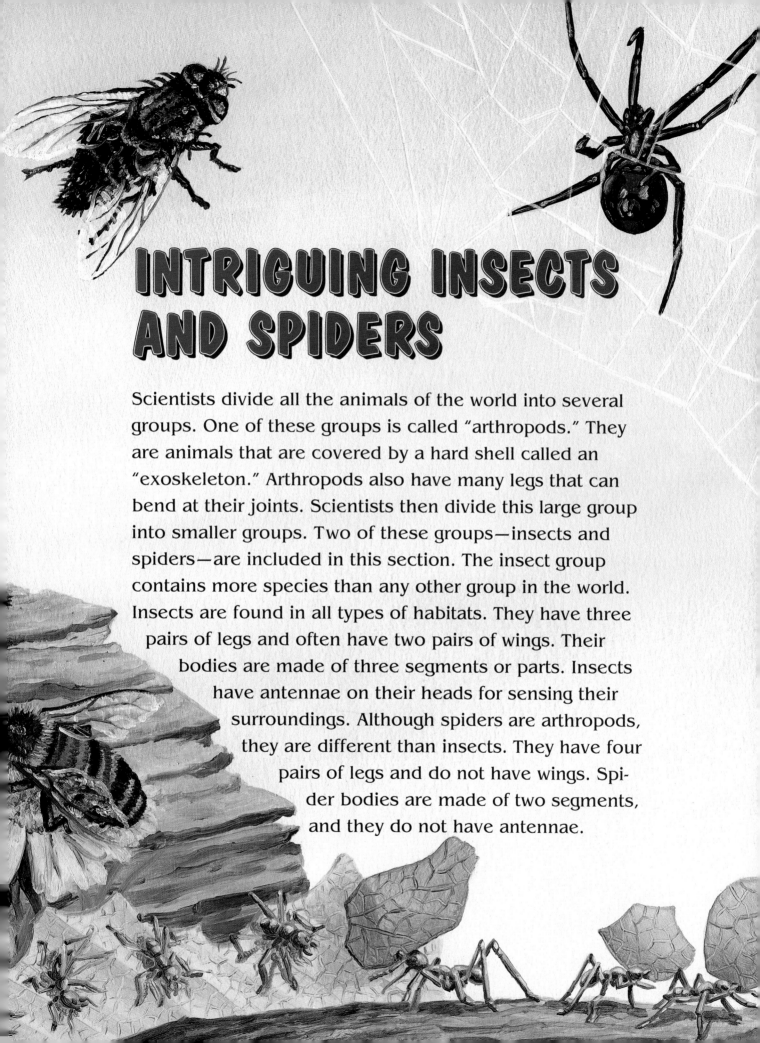

INTRIGUING INSECTS AND SPIDERS

Scientists divide all the animals of the world into several groups. One of these groups is called "arthropods." They are animals that are covered by a hard shell called an "exoskeleton." Arthropods also have many legs that can bend at their joints. Scientists then divide this large group into smaller groups. Two of these groups—insects and spiders—are included in this section. The insect group contains more species than any other group in the world. Insects are found in all types of habitats. They have three pairs of legs and often have two pairs of wings. Their bodies are made of three segments or parts. Insects have antennae on their heads for sensing their surroundings. Although spiders are arthropods, they are different than insects. They have four pairs of legs and do not have wings. Spider bodies are made of two segments, and they do not have antennae.

Butterflies and Moths

Butterflies and moths are insects. They have three pairs of legs, a pair of wings, three body segments, and antennae. More than 150,000 species of butterflies and moths have been found throughout the world, most commonly in warm climates. Unlike other insects, butterflies and moths have tiny scales. The scales on their bodies look furry. The scales on their wings are flat and overlap one another. If you look closely at a butterfly, you'll see that its wings shimmer. It's the scales that make this sparkle. Adult butterflies and moths feed on flower nectar and fruit juice. They have special mouth parts that are long and hollow, like a straw. They unroll the straw to feed and roll it back up to fly. Young butterflies and moths look quite different from adults. They are called "caterpillars." They use their jaws to eat leaves and other plant parts. Butterflies and moths go through a life cycle called "metamorphosis."

Painted Lady The painted lady butterfly is one of the most common butterflies in America and Europe. During the breeding season, females travel hundreds of miles to lay their eggs.

Monarch Monarch butterflies have beautiful black and orange wings. When they eat milkweed, they absorb poison into their bodies. This makes them taste bad to birds and other predators.

Zebra Swallowtail (below) As you can see, zebra swallowtails are named for their zebralike color pattern. Their predators have a hard time seeing them. Swallowtails have long tails on their hindwings.

Cabbage White

Cecropia Moth (right) Cecropia moths live only about two weeks. That's because adults cannot eat! They are born without a mouth. Their only purpose is to mate and lay eggs.

Metamorphosis: The butterfly life cycle

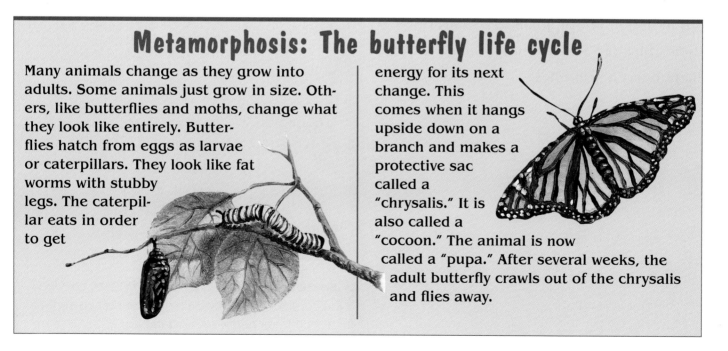

Many animals change as they grow into adults. Some animals just grow in size. Others, like butterflies and moths, change what they look like entirely. Butterflies hatch from eggs as larvae or caterpillars. They look like fat worms with stubby legs. The caterpillar eats in order to get energy for its next change. This comes when it hangs upside down on a branch and makes a protective sac called a "chrysalis." It is also called a "cocoon." The animal is now called a "pupa." After several weeks, the adult butterfly crawls out of the chrysalis and flies away.

Dragonflies and Damselflies

About 5,000 species of dragonflies and damselflies have been found throughout the world. Like other insects, they have three body parts: the head, the thorax, and the abdomen. The head of a dragonfly or damselfly is easy to see because of its large eyes. Right behind the head is a fat section where the wings attach. This is the thorax. The long, often striped taillike part is the abdomen. Both dragonflies and damselflies begin their lives in the water. They hatch from eggs and look like small adults without wings. They are called "nymphs." Dragonfly nymphs are predators and attack small water animals. Damselfly nymphs eat tiny plants. As adults, dragonflies and damselflies look different. Dragonflies are larger and have a fat abdomen. Damselflies are smaller and have a thin abdomen. Dragonflies usually hold their wings out when resting. Damselflies fold them over their bodies.

Green Darner Dragonfly This green darner is one of the largest species of dragonflies in North America. Its eyes meet in the middle of its head and give it an all-around view.

Common Blue Damselfly This common blue damselfly may look delicate, but it can survive as far north as northern Scotland.

Grasshoppers, Crickets, Stick Insects, and Cockroaches

About 20,000 species of grasshoppers and crickets are found throughout the world (except the Arctic and Antarctica) and are especially diverse in the tropics. Grasshoppers and crickets have strong back legs that they use for jumping. Most have two pairs of wings—the forewings and hind wings. The forewings are tough and protect the hind wings. The thin hind wings are used for flying. Male grasshoppers and crickets use sounds to attract a female. They make a chirping sound by rubbing two body parts together like their legs or wings. Young grasshoppers and crickets are called "hoppers."

There are 2,000 species of stick insect in the world. Some have wings, but most do not. They live in plants and use camouflage to protect themselves from predators. Stick insects even lay camouflaged eggs that look like small seeds.

About 4,000 types of cockroaches live in the world. They usually live on the ground and rarely use their wings for flight. Cockroaches are active at night and will eat just about anything, including soap. Cockroaches leave a bad smell wherever they go.

Cave Cricket Cave or camel crickets are sometimes unwanted visitors in house basements. Normally they live in caves or dark places like under logs. Cave crickets have very large drumstick-shape legs.

Walking Stick Walking sticks camouflage themselves in the branches of plants. Some even have body parts that look like thorns or leaves.

Grasshoppers, Crickets, Stick Insects, and Cockroaches

Preying Mantis
Preying mantises usually eat their prey while the prey are still alive. Female mantises often eat the males during mating. They are also known as "praying" mantises because they look as if they are kneeling.

American Cockroach Cockroaches are fast runners. They like the dark and scurry away if someone turns on a light. They are unwanted visitors in homes because they carry diseases.

Two-striped Grasshopper

Hiding from enemies

Insects can avoid predators by using camouflage. They blend in with their surroundings so that they're hard to see. The gum leaf grasshopper, for example, looks just like the leaf of a eucalyptus tree. Walking leaf insects have bodies shaped like leaves. Another defense against predators is mimicry. Mimicry is when one animal is shaped or colored to look like a harmful animal. A hoverfly has the same colorings as a wasp but is unable to sting. Moths often have large "eyespots" on their wings. They mimic the eyes of a larger animal, such as an owl or a hawk.

Cracker butterfly

Twig mantis

Green walking stick

Leaf mimic katydid

Bees and Wasps

Bees and wasps are insects. Their bodies are divided into three sections. Bees and wasps have four thin wings for flying and six legs for walking. Bees usually have fuzzy bodies while wasps are smooth. Both bees and wasps are social animals. This means they live in large family groups. Each member of the family, or colony, has a specific job. Most bees get their food from flowers. Wasps can eat wood, fruit, and plant parts. Both bees and wasps have special body parts called "stingers." They are found at the ends of their abdomens and are used for protection. Stingers inject poison into another animal's body. Bees have hooks on their stingers. This makes it hard for the predator to pull out. Usually, the stinger gets so stuck that it is pulled out of the bee's body. Because of this, bees can sting only once and die right afterward. Wasps have stingers that are sharp and smooth. They can sting a predator over and over again.

Honeybee Honeybees use baskets on their back legs for collecting pollen. Pollen is used to make honey. In the winter, bees use the honey for food.

Paper Wasp Paper wasps chew wood and mix it with saliva. They spit it out and use it to build their round nests.

Hornet Hornets are larger than most wasps. They eat nectar but also hunt insects. Hornets cut off the head and legs of their prey before taking it back to their nest.

Yellow Jacket

Beetles

About 300,000 types of beetles live in the world, which is about one-third of the entire group of insects! Beetles live on land and in fresh water. They eat a variety of foods, including pollen, leaves, wool, and animal waste. Just like other insects, beetles have a hard outer covering called an "exoskeleton," which protects their insides. When beetles fly, you can see that they have one pair of wings called "hind wings." Also sticking out are body parts that look like wings, but they're hard. These are called "elytra." Elytra cover and protect the hind wings when the beetle isn't flying. Beetles also go through a metamorphosis when they're born. Their bodies change many times before they're adults. Beetles come in many sizes and shapes.

Ladybird Beetle Ladybird beetles are commonly called "ladybugs." They are one of the most useful insects for gardens because they eat aphids and other plant pests.

Stag Beetle Male stag beetles have large jaws shaped like horns or antlers. They use them during the breeding season to fight other males.

Dung Beetle Dung beetles are named for their diet. They find animal droppings, roll a portion of it into a ball, roll the ball away, and bury it as food for their young.

Firefly Male and female fireflies make flashes of light to find a mate. Males flash their lights as they fly above the ground, and females on the ground flash back to them.

Japanese Beetle These colorful beetles are a serious threat to plants and crops. Even the larvae, which live underground, can cause damage when they feed.

Insects and farmers

Most insects feed on plants. They might chew on the leaves, suck on fruit nectar, or use pollen from flowers to create honey. When humans began growing their own food, they quickly developed relationships with insects. Some insects damage crops by eating too much of the plant. Aphids, for example, are known to destroy entire crops by sucking the sap from the plants. It does not help that female aphids can give birth to babies several times in one day. Other insects are helpful to the farmers. The ladybird beetle, commonly called the "ladybug," eats aphids and other plant pests.

Termites

The 1,800 species of termites can be found throughout the world as far north as Toronto and are quite diverse in the tropics. Just like ants, bees, and wasps, termites are social insects. This means they live in large family groups. These groups are called "colonies." There can be millions of termites in one colony! Three types of termites live together within each colony—the queen, the workers, and the soldiers. The queen's job is to lay the eggs. All her needs are taken care of by the other termites. The workers clean the nest, find food, and take care of the young. Soldiers protect the nest from predators. Normally, termites do not have wings. During the breeding season, some young are born with wings. They leave the nest to begin new colonies.

African Savanna Termite The African savanna termite queen is so large that she cannot leave her room! Worker termites take care of her while she lays up to 30,000 eggs a day.

Termite

Structure of termite mounds

African savanna termites build giant nests that can reach more than 18 feet high. Worker termites build the mounds by mixing soil with their saliva. They spit it out and let it harden in the sun. Most of the termites are not found in this tall part of the nest. They are found underground in long tunnels and special rooms. The queen has her own room. Another room holds the colony's food, and still another is for the young. The mound above ground has hundreds of tunnels, chimneys, and vent holes. They control the airflow and temperature of the nest.

Tree Termite The nests of tree termites can be on the ground or up high. They are made of feces and saliva. Soldier termites use a turpentinelike secretion from their heads to defend the nest.

Flies, Mosquitoes, and Fleas

Flies are different from other insects because they have only one pair of wings. Instead of hind wings, they have small body parts called "halteres," which help the flies keep their balance during flight. Flies are able to hover, take off quickly, and even land upside down. This makes them hard to catch. Flies have special mouthparts for feeding on liquids. Some can pierce and suck their food while others use a spongelike mouth for soaking up fluids. The 3,000 species of mosquitoes belong to the fly family. Male mosquitoes feed on flower nectar, but females use their sharp mouthparts to suck up blood from other animals. Adult fleas also feed on animal blood. Fleas do not have wings. They get from one animal to another by jumping. Jumping is what they are famous for as well as carrying diseases.

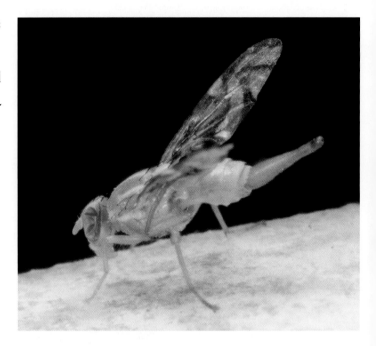

Pomace or Fruit Fly

Horsefly Female horseflies feed on blood. They cut their victim's skin and then suck up the blood as it oozes out. Male horseflies eat nectar and pollen.

Housefly Houseflies are probably the most common insects on earth. They feed on sweet and rotten things. Their tongues are like tiny sponges that soak up liquid.

Common Flea The most common flea is the cat flea. It has sharp mouthparts and powerful back legs. Their bodies are narrow so they can walk in between hairs and feathers.

Rat Flea It is believed rat fleas carried the illness that caused the Black Death from A.D. 1347 to 1351. The Black Death was one of the worst plagues in history.

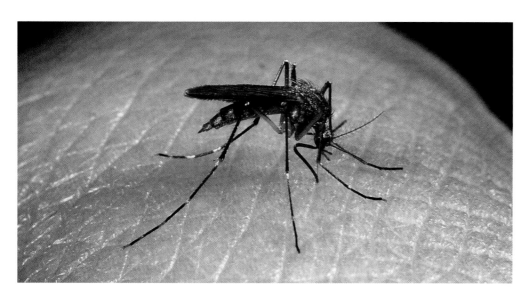

Mosquito Female mosquitoes have sharp, needlelike mouths for sucking blood. Mosquitoes can be dangerous because they carry diseases.

Insect homes

Insects can be found on land, in freshwater, and in the air. The only place they cannot survive is in the ocean. They make their homes in a variety of places. Some insects live on plants, such as walking sticks. Their body shapes camouflage them from predators. The giant water bug lives in freshwater where it eats tadpoles and salamanders. Other insects, like the burying beetle, can be found underground. They bury small dead animals, like a mouse, build their nest over it, and let their young eat it when they hatch. Insects like ticks and fleas make their homes on the bodies of other animals.

Spiders

Spiders are grouped together with scorpions, mites, and ticks in a group known as "arachnids." They are the second largest group of animals on the planet. Spiders are different than insects in a number of ways. They have bodies that have two sections instead of three. Spiders have four pairs of legs (eight legs total) instead of three (six legs total). Spiders do not have antennae or wings. Of the 35,000 species of spiders, all are carnivorous. This means they eat other animals. They do this with fangs that inject poisonous venom into their prey. Some spiders have large fangs and can be dangerous to humans. Others, like the garden spider, are not a threat to humans. Most spiders have four pairs of eyes, but their eyesight is poor. They usually hunt by touch. Hairs on their bodies and legs sense their environment and possible prey. Spiders use special body parts for making silk. Silk is a strong thread that spiders use to make a web, protect their eggs, trap their food, and travel with.

Daddy Longlegs It's easy to see how the daddy longlegs got its name! Daddy longlegs are often seen inside homes hanging upside down on their web.

Wolf Spider Wolf spiders rarely make webs. They walk on the ground hunting for prey. Female wolf spiders wrap their eggs in sacs and carry them as they hunt.

Tarantula Tarantulas are large spiders with special fangs that point down. After injecting their venom, the fangs can hold the prey down while the tarantula eats it.

Black Widow Spider Black widows have a red hour-glass-shape pattern under their abdomens. Female black widows often eat the male after mating.

Is a spider an insect?

Scientists group animals together based on certain body shapes and parts. Animals that have six legs, a pair of antennae, and a body made of three parts are grouped together as insects. If you look closely at a spider, certain insect features are missing. Spiders have four pairs of legs. Spiders do not have antennae. They use hairs on their bodies to sense their surroundings. Spiders have bodies that are made of two main parts: the cephalothorax, which is the head and chest together, and the abdomen. So, spiders are not insects. They are grouped together as arachnids.

Jumping Spider

Ants

Ants come in a variety of colors and sizes. Their bodies have three sections. The first is a large head with long, bendable antennae. The thorax is next and holds most of the ant's body parts. The largest body section is the abdomen. It holds the ant's digestive and reproductive parts. Some ants have a stinger at the end of their abdomens. Ants do not usually have wings, but some species grow wings during the breeding season. Ants are social animals. This means they live in family groups called "colonies." The diet of ants differs from one species to another. Some are vegetarians and eat only plants. Some hunt other small animals. Most are scavengers and collect food wherever they can find it.

Leaf-cutting Ants Leaf-cutting ants take pieces of leaves to their nests. In a special chamber, they let the leaves decay. The ants eat the fungus that grows on the leaves.

Safari Ant Large safari ants can swarm and quickly eat a large animal. They bury their heads into the flesh and won't let go even if their heads are pulled from their bodies!

Fire Ant Fire ants use stingers for protection. The poison they inject causes a blister and can hurt for several hours.

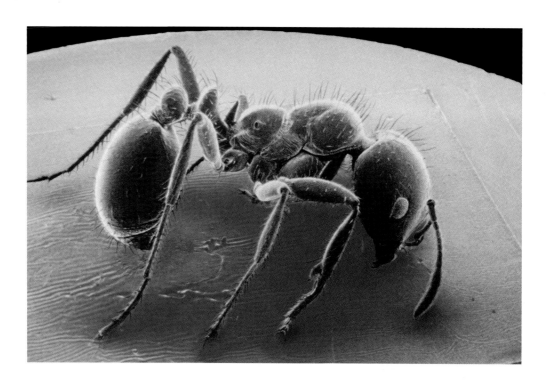

Ant jobs

Ants are social insects, which means they live in colonies or family groups. There are three types of ants in a colony—a queen, workers, and soldiers. The queen is the only one who can lay eggs. She is usually much larger than the other ants. Worker ants build the nest, take care of the queen, find and collect food, and care for the young. Soldier ants protect the colony from predators. They usually have special body parts for this. Some have large jaws for biting predators. Others can spray stinging poisons.

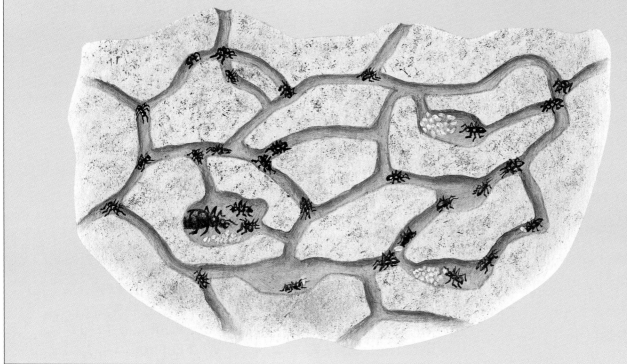

INDEX OF ANIMAL SUBGROUPS